Cicerone County Walking Series

WALKING
IN
BUCKINGHAMSHIRE

Cicerone County Walking Series

Cicerone County Walking Series

WALKING
IN
BUCKINGHAMSHIRE

by

Robert J. Wilson

CICERONE PRESS
MILNTHORPE, CUMBRIA, UK
www.cicerone.co.uk

A catalogue record for this book is available from the British Library.

Advice to Readers

Readers are advised that while every effort is taken by the author to ensure the accuracy of this guidebook, changes can occur which may affect the contents. It is advisable to check locally on transport, accommodation, shops, etc, but even rights of way can be altered.

The publisher would welcome notes of any such changes.

Front cover: Autumnal scenes at the beechwoods near Fingest

CONTENTS

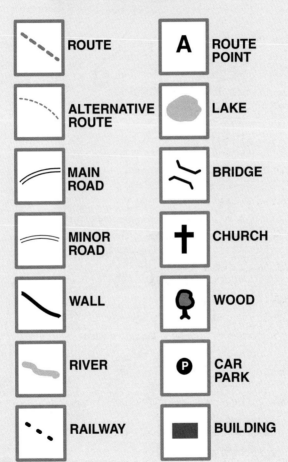

KEY TO MAPS

ROUTE		**A**	ROUTE POINT
ALTERNATIVE ROUTE			LAKE
MAIN ROAD			BRIDGE
MINOR ROAD		**†**	CHURCH
WALL			WOOD
RIVER		**P**	CAR PARK
RAILWAY			BUILDING

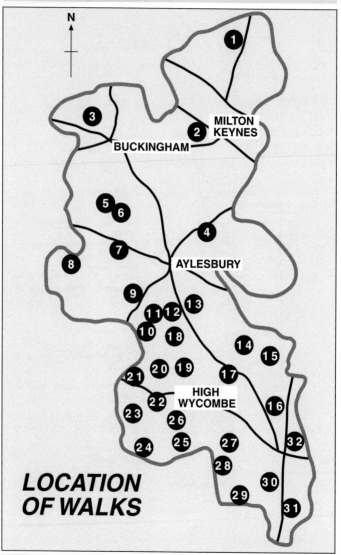

LOCATION
OF WALKS

INTRODUCTION

While the landscape of Buckinghamshire, the long, narrow county
linking the Midlands with London, is not one of dramatic contrasts,
its pretty villages, pastoral farmland, rolling hills and peaceful beechwoods have a particular 'homely' appeal. The walks in this guidebook cover the wide spectrum of the Buckinghamshire landscape –
from the lush water meadows around Olney and the Ouse Valley in
the north, through the Vale of Aylesbury to the Chilterns, and finally
through south Buckinghamshire to the Colne Valley by the western
edge of Greater London.

Around Olney the scenery is typically Midland, with stone
cottages and the large stone spire of Olney church, which is of typical
Northamptonshire design. The Vale of Aylesbury consists of pastoral
farmland with pretty villages. Although the soil north of the Chilterns
is clay based, the clay is mixed with glacial material which makes for
better drainage (and easier walking) than the heavy London clay
found in the extreme southeastern corner of the county. In recent
years the quality of the footpaths in the Vale has been much improved
and makes for pleasant walking, especially in the warm summer
months.

For walkers, though, the jewel in the Buckinghamshire crown is
still the Chilterns, with deep-sided valleys (somewhat deeper in the
south), brick and flint cottages, and beechwoods. The beechwoods in
autumn are a glorious sight, the summer greens giving way to a
symphony of browns, oranges and yellows. Autumn is one of the best
times for walking, too, as the ground is usually still reasonably dry
and the temperature at a comfortable level for walking. In the
summer, the heavy leaf cover in the beechwoods provides a
welcoming shade when the sun is strongest.

Southeast of the Wye Valley the landscape changes again, with a
plateau gently sloping down towards the Thames. In the extreme
southeast of the county are the Misbourne and Colne Valleys, where
the chalk hills give way to London clay. On the county border is the
Colne Valley Park, the first extensive stretch of countryside reached
when leaving London westwards. The Grand Union Canal marks the
end of Buckinghamshire and the start of the London borough of

The churchyard and cottages at Turville, one of the prettiest villages in the Chilterns (see Walk 13)

Hillingdon. Walking along the canal towpaths is a different experience again: there is an aura of peace and quiet despite an urban feel to the walk in places.

Maps

The whole of the county is covered by the Ordnance Survey Landranger maps, sheets 152, 165, 175 and 176. Most of the county (south of Milton Keynes) is now covered by the new OS Explorer series, which is replacing the old Pathfinder series. The relevant Explorer sheets are 171, 172, 180, 181 and 192. These maps are of a larger scale (1:25,000) and show the field boundaries (particularly useful in north Buckinghamshire).

The sketch maps in the book are designed only to give the walker a general impression of the route and to enable the walk to be traced on the relevant Ordance Survey sheet. Walkers are strongly recommended to take the relevant Ordance Survey map with them as well as the guidebook.

Note: The parking symbol on the sketch maps indicates a purpose-built car park.

Notes on using the guide

The walks in this book are all between 4 and 10 miles, and are well within the capabilities of the average walker. Walking in Buckinghamshire does not require any specialist equipment, although a trekking pole is useful on some of the steeper Chiltern slopes.

Each route description opens with a brief fact file, which states the distance, typical time taken, relevant OS maps, the start point and details of refreshments en route (if any). Background information is given in italics at the relevant point in the route description.

Various recreational paths have been created by Buckinghamshire County Council – the Midshires Way (across north Buckinghamshire), the Swan's Way (across the vale beneath the Chiltern escarpment), the North Bucks Way (north from the Ridgeway across the Vale of Aylesbury), the South Bucks Way (along the Misbourne Valley from Denham to Coombe Hill via the Hampden Country), the Chess Valley Walk (east from Chesham) and the Chiltern Link (from Chesham to Wendover, linking the Chess Valley Walk and the Ridgeway). The Ridgeway Path is the only National Trail (formerly designated a Long Distance Footpath) passing through Buckinghamshire. It features in Walks 10, 11, 12, 13 and 18.

The paths are generally well waymarked, especially in the Chilterns, where the Chiltern Society has carried out an extensive waymarking programme (white arrows on trees) for some years. All over the county, Buckinghamshire County Council has carried out a waymarking programme in recent years using the standard yellow waymarks for footpaths and blue arrows for bridleways (the bridleways are easier to follow but can be exceptionally muddy after rain).

Where the path crosses farmland, PLEASE keep to the path. Remember that the farmer has to make a living out of the land you are walking across.

Most of the walks have pubs en route and there are still plenty of village stores in which to stock up. All the pubs offer excellent bar meals (although some may not be open every weekday lunchtime). Stowe, Claydon House and Cliveden also offer excellent teas. The tea room at Stowe and the restaurant at Cliveden also offer lunches, and the Cliveden restrauant menu contains a fine range of vegetarian meals. The tea room at Claydon House is in one of the outbuildings, so you don't have to go inside the house for refreshments.

Access

The railways from London stop at Aylesbury, and while the level of service provided is fairly reliable, it is still easier to reach the start of the walks by car. Main roads radiate out across the county from London, and while these are often busy, once drivers are on the minor roads leading to the villages the route becomes increasingly country-fied. Parking – either in car parks, off-road parking spots or quiet roads wide enough for traffic to pass – is generally not a problem, but please be considerate to the locals. The bus service is sporadic, and in some cases cannot be relied upon to transport you to the walk and back again in the same day. If you are intending to use the buses, it is advisable to make enquiries before you travel. The Buckinghamshire Traveline telephone enquiry service is open from 7am to 8pm (8am to 8pm at weekends). The number is 0870 608 2608, calls being charged at the local rate.

People and the landscape

In each of the villages the central building is the church, many of which were renovated in the 19th century. Most churches are usually open, but those in the smallest or busiest places are kept locked. Many publish guide booklets for a modest price (and in buying a guide book you are contributing to the costs of maintaining the building).

The Vale of Aylesbury contains several ornate stately homes, some built by the Rothschilds, the wealthy banking dynasty. Their influence is also felt in the neighbouring villages, notably Waddesdon, in the shadow of Waddesdon Manor. Near to Wing is the more restrained Ascott House. Both Waddesdon Manor and Ascott House are now owned by the National Trust. Halton House, nestling beneath Wendover Woods, is not open to the public, being part of RAF Halton. Near Wing is Wingrave, a village with some Rothschild-designed buildings, but no separate manor.

West Wycombe is the domain of the Dashwoods, who live at West Wycombe House (also National Trust). Their famous family head was Sir Francis, who built the Hell Fire Caves and the mausoleum on the hill opposite.

High above the Thames is Cliveden House, formerly the home of the Astor family. It is now owned by the National Trust, although the house itself has been converted into a luxury hotel. The extensive grounds – including the hanging woods leading down to the river, formal parterre and water garden – make for relaxed walks. The estate was central to the Profumo affair in the early 1960s.

The area east of Amersham and Chesham is part of 'Metroland', the name given to the commuter belt that developed along the Metropolitan railway line into London and the suburbs that grew up around the stations. In the early part of the 20th century, the chairman of the Metropolitan railway, Sir Edward Watkin, had dreams of Metroland extending out into the Vale of Aylesbury to Quainton Junction and Brill. Thankfully this never happened, as the distance and (even then) the fares involved in commuting into London were prohibitive. Today the Metropolitan line stops at Amersham, though the Chiltern line from Marylebone still runs to Aylesbury.

Cropping up all over the Chilterns is an earthwork called Grim's Ditch. These are not sections of one long earthwork, but separate ones. The ditches are named after the Norse god Grimr, who liked to remain anonymous and was called Grimr by the people because no one knew his real name. As no one knew who built these earthworks, they were named after the unknown god.

WALK 1 – OLNEY

DISTANCE:	**16km/10 miles**
TIME:	**4 hours**
MAP:	**OS Landranger 152**
START:	**Car park next to the recreation ground (Grid Ref 891516)**
REFRESHMENTS:	**The Swan pub, Sherington; pubs, cafes and shops, Olney**

The walk starts from Olney, the northernmost town in Buckinghamshire, only a few miles from the Northamptonshire border. There are no steep climbs, but plenty of wide views. After passing through Emberton Country Park, the walk crosses farmland to the pretty villages of Filgrave, Sherington and Emberton before returning to Olney (pronounced O-ney).

START: The large public car park next to the recreation ground on the eastern edge of the town (grid ref 891516). The car park is signposted from the main street. Limited parking is also available in the Market Square and along the northern end of the High Street. Olney is reached from Junction 14 of the M1 by heading north on the A509 (away from Milton Keynes). Buses from Bedford and Northampton stop at Olney.

Olney High Street has maintained its country town character, with various different small shops, a wine bar and several pubs. In the spring time the Market Square has an impressive flower collection. In the 18th century, Olney was the home of John Newton, a slave trader turned vicar, and the poet William Cowper. Together they produced the Olney Hymns, the most famous of which is 'Amazing Grace'. Today, Olney is most famous for its pancake race on Shrove Tuesday, which is run between the Market Square and the church. The women of the town dress up in an apron and bonnet, and run holding a frying pan and pancake, which they must toss three times during the race. It all started in the 15th century when a housewife heard the bells for

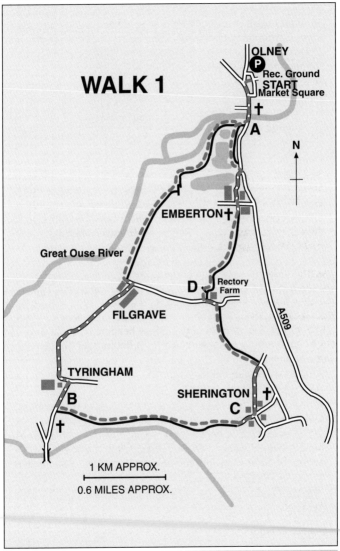

WALK 1

OLNEY
P
Rec. Ground
START
Market Square
†
A

N

EMBERTON †

Great Ouse River

D Rectory Farm

FILGRAVE

A509

TYRINGHAM

B †

SHERINGTON †

C

1 KM APPROX.

0.6 MILES APPROX.

the Shrove Tuesday service in the middle of cooking a pancake, so rushed off to church still holding the frying pan and pancake. Olney Church, with its tall stone spire, looks more like a Northamptonshire design, as do the stone cottages in Olney and the surrounding villages.

THE WALK: Turn left out of the car park, then right along an alleyway, passing the Cowper memorial church to reach the High Street. Turn left along the High Street past the Market Square and the church. After crossing the River Ouse, turn right **(A)** through a kissing gate, with an avenue of trees on your left. At the far end turn left to merge with a metalled track which is part of Emberton Country Park.

The Emberton Country Park was created out of a series of disused gravel pits which were created during the construction of the nearby M1. There is a nature reserve and areas for boating, as well as a metalled track round the lakes – popular for family days out.

Follow the public bridleway waymarks round the park. After passing a children's playground, turn right into a caravan park. At a T-junction turn left. After only a few yards, thankfully, turn right by a waymark post through a bridlegate. The track is well defined and rises gently across the field to a hedge gap. Continue along a track (now between fields). There are wide views all around. Ignore all turnings off, and reach Manor Farm in the hamlet of Filgrave. At the farm turn left to reach a lane at a right-angled bend. Turn right through a gate and continue straight on along the lane past some attractive cottages on the left. After 2km (about 1½ miles) Tyringham is reached. Later join the Three Shires Way (keep to road).

Tyringham is not a village as such, just a mansion and grounds, built by the architect Sir John Soane (who also designed the Bank of England) at the end of the 18th century, together with a church hidden behind trees. A short detour brings you to the bridge across the River Ouse and the gateway, also built by Soane and remaining unaltered.

(B) At a public bridleway sign, turn left through a gate and cross the field (the church is behind some trees on your right). Pass through a gate in the field corner, then continue along the left-hand edge of the next field. On reaching a large field, bear right to reach the right-hand edge of this field (also the river bank). Go through a gate in the corner and continue past a windmill. Follow the right-hand side of a series of fields, then continue along a track and lane (ignoring all turnings off) leading into Sherington. The village and church are visible ahead.

Sherington is an attractive village, consisting of cottages and farm buildings centered around a village green, with a pub and a couple of shops. The Swan is an ideal place to stop for a break, especially after the Tyringham to Sherington stretch, which can be heavy going after a wet winter. The church, in the northeastern corner of the village, is a dominant landmark in the surrounding area.

(C) Turn left at the cross-roads by the village green, past the shops. The Swan pub is on the right. Just after passing Gun Lane turn left over a stile by a public footpath sign. Again, the path is well defined and follows the left-hand edge of the field. After a rise the path descends, then swings right in a dip, climbing gently again. Looking back, there is a fine view back towards Woburn. At the top of the rise cross over a track to rejoin the Three Shires Way, along by a strip of woodland on your left. Ahead there is a fine view towards Olney and Emberton. Turn left along a lane, then right along a bridleway (still the Three Shires Way) when the lane begins to drop **(D)**. At the farmhouse continue along by a fence on your left.

At a bridlegate bear right across the meadow, following a yellow waymark arrow to reach a stile and continuing on across the next field (path well defined) towards Olney church ahead. The path bears right across the next field to a footbridge in the field corner. Turn right along the bottom edge of the next field, with a stream on your left. At a yellow waymark, turn left across a footbridge and on across the next field (path well defined again). Cross two meadows by a series of stiles to reach the village of Emberton. Continue down a side road. At a T-junction turn left past the Bull and Bear.

Emberton has been quiet since the village bypass opened in the 1970s. In the middle of the village is a clock tower designed with pinnacles and lancets as a mini church tower. It was built as a memorial to a rector's wife in 1846 and named Margaret's Tower. It is now the village war memorial.

At the clock tower turn right along Olney Road. Just before the main road is reached, turn left into Emberton Country Park (walkers don't have to pay to go in). Turn right along the drive signposted to the Sailing Club, with the lakes on your left. Where the track bends left at the northern end of the lakes, continue straight on past the flood bridge to the kissing gate where you entered the park at the start of the walk. Turn left along the road, returning to Olney. Retrace your steps back to the start.

WALK 2 – WHADDON CHASE

DISTANCE:	12km/7½ miles
TIME:	3 hours
MAP:	OS Landranger 152
START:	Waddon Village (Grid Ref 806341)
REFRESHMENTS:	Lowndes Arms, Whaddon; Old Crown pub, Little Horwood

From the village of Whaddon, the walk crosses a pleasant pinewood before following a section of the Swan's Way. After passing underneath the main A421, the walk crosses farmland to reach the village of Little Horwood, soon passing Little Horwood Manor. The climax of the walk is a traverse across Whaddon Chase, with fine views all around to return to Whaddon.

START: The village of Whaddon (grid ref 806341). There is on-road parking along the main street southeast of the church. Whaddon is reached from Milton Keynes by proceeding westwards along the A421 and turning right along a minor road signposted to Whaddon. Buses stop in the villages of Little Horwood and Whaddon.

THE WALK: In the village of Whaddon, head northwest along the main street towards the church. Turn right by a public footpath sign. A bridlegate at the back of the Lowndes Arms pub car park leads to the footpath out of the village, past Whaddon Hall.

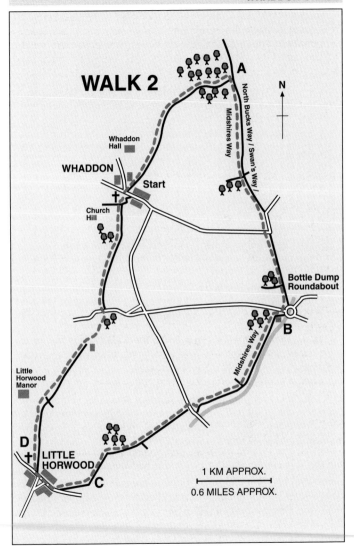

WALK 2

A

N

North Bucks Way / Swan's Way

Midshires Way

Whaddon Hall

WHADDON

Start

Church Hill

Bottle Dump Roundabout

B

Midshires Way

Little Horwood Manor

D

LITTLE HORWOOD

C

1 KM APPROX.

0.6 MILES APPROX.

Whaddon Hall was built on the site of the former manor house of the Selby-Lowndes family. The present house is a plain brick mansion built in 1820, although the north side features some Ionic columns.

Bear right through a kissing gate, and continue along by a fence on your left. Where the fence bends left, go straight on across the field to a stile and carry on down the next field. Whaddon Hall is on your left. At the bottom, continue round the left-hand edge of the next field, passing round the hillock ahead. After the next stile, turn right (following a waymark arrow) to a stile leading into Oakhill Wood. Follow the path straight on through this pleasant pinewood, climbing gently.

(A) On the far side of the wood, turn right onto the Swan's Way (a long-distance bridleway)/Midshires Way, along the right-hand edge of the field (wood on right). Later the path swings left (now between fences). Continue straight on, where the South Bucks Way joins the track, and keep going straight on when a road is reached. This road passes along the boundary of Milton Keynes, although you are still in the heart of the countryside.

Where the road bends right, continue straight on along the track by a bridleway sign. Ignore all turnings off. Later the path descends to pass under the A421. After passing under the main road, turn right along a track.

(B) Just before the main road turn left, passing some stables. On reaching open countryside bear left across the field to reach a bridlegate (NOT the track straight on alongside the wood). Continue across two further fields via bridlegates to reach the corner of the field next to a stream. Follow the path alongside the stream, ignoring a bridleway going off to the right. Later the path bends right, then left to a bridlegate. Here, bear left across the field to a bridlegate, following a blue waymark, and onto a road.

Turn right along this road for a few yards, then turn left across the field by a public bridleway sign. Make for the right-hand end of the hedge and line of trees ahead. Continue across the next field to the field corner ahead. Bear left to a bridlegate and carry on alongside the wood ahead. At the far side of the wood, pass through a gate and follow the edge of the field round to a bridlegate in the opposite field corner. **(C)** After passing through a second bridlegate, bear right across a large field to a bridlegate in the opposite field corner. After crossing the next field continue along the right-hand edge of a further field to reach Little Horwood. Turn left along a lane, then right along a road passing the Old Crown pub.

Little Horwood is an attractive village built around winding roads. The church of St. Nicholas was heavily restored in 1889. Inside there is a wall-painting depicting the Seven Deadly Sins. The painting is now rather faint, but the main figure is a bearded man with scrolls symbolising 'Pride'. Six branches are growing out of his body, each with a monster's head on the end representing the other six sins. The main painting in the church is 'Christ and the Sheep', with Jesus as the Good Shepherd. It is by a Spanish painter, Don Alonzo Pobar, whose style is similar to Murillo's.

Little Horwood Manor (see below) was built in 1938, one of the last stately homes to be built in England. It was built in a Lutyenesque style, with a centre with a pyramid roof and wings with pavillions and pyramid roofs.

(D) Turn right by a public footpath sign just before the church. Cross the eastern edge of the churchyard (fence on right) past the village school. Cross a playing field to a stile in the field corner. Continue along the right-hand edge of a series of fields. Little Horwood Manor is on your left. Where the hedge bends right carry straight on across the field to a stile ahead, and on along the right-hand edge of the next field. Cross over a stile in the fence and continue round the left-hand edge of the next field to a further stile, maintaining the same direction as before. The path goes round a thicket with a pond. Continue across the next field via a series of stiles. After crossing a track, continue along the left-hand edge of the next field, alongside a ditch on your left. Continue through scrub to a footbridge and stile in the corner, then cross the next field to a stile in the opposite fence, climbing gently, passing a pond. Cross over a drive and bear left across the next field to a stile by a gate. Turn right along a minor road, and just before the A421 bear right onto a cycle track signposted to Whaddon. Cross the road to a public footpath sign by a stile. Bear right to a stile in the opposite fence (Whaddon church ahead).

Whaddon Chase is an area of wide fields and fox coverts between Whaddon and Little Horwood. A 'chase' is a detached part of a former royal forest, and Whaddon was granted this status by Henry III. Originally covering a larger part of north Buckinghamshire, Whaddon Chase is classic hunting country, and there are fine views all around.

Pass through a gate and continue along a track between fields (later with a hedge on your right). Cross over track, pass through a gate opposite and continue along the right-hand edge of the next field, climbing gently. Pass through a bridlegate, past a covert. There are wide views left and right. Follow the right-hand edge of the fields until you reach Whaddon church. Turn right onto the path along the edge of the churchyard, passing to the right of the church. Go through a gate and carry on down the lane into the village. Turn left along the road to return to your starting point.

WALK 3 – STOWE LANDSCAPE GARDENS

DISTANCE:	**6km/4 miles**
TIME:	**2 hours**
MAP:	**OS Landranger 152; National Trust Stowe visitor information leaflet**
START:	**National Trust car park at Stowe (Grid Ref 674376)**
REFRESHMENTS:	**Tea rooms, Stowe Gardens**

A walk with a difference – a gentle stroll round Stowe Landscape Gardens, created in the grounds of a mansion (later Stowe School) over a 150 year period from 1700 by William Kent and, later, 'Capability' Brown. It is an epic landscape garden – one of the largest in Europe – with various monuments, temples, and the like. The National Trust embarked on an ambitious conservation project when it acquired the gardens in 1989 and opened them to the public. The house is still occupied by Stowe School.

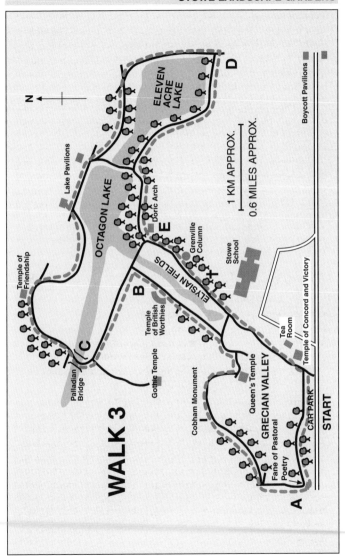

WALK 3

N

Temple of Friendship
Palladian Bridge
Lake Pavilions
OCTAGON LAKE
ELEVEN ACRE LAKE
Boycott Pavilions
Doric Arch
Grenville Column
Stowe School
Gothic Temple
Temple of British Worthies
ELYSIAN FIELDS
Cobham Monument
GRECIAN VALLEY
Fane of Pastoral Poetry
Queen's Temple
Tea Room
Temple of Concord and Victory
CAR PARK
START

A B C D E

1 KM APPROX.
0.6 MILES APPROX.

START: Stowe Gardens National Trust car park (grid ref 674376). Stowe is signposted from Buckingham along the long approach of Stowe Avenue. The gardens are open every day in the school holidays, and Monday, Wednesday, Friday and Sunday in term time (except January–March). Opening times vary from year to year (tel. 01280 822850 for information). Buses from Aylesbury and Milton Keynes stop in Buckingham. A large-scale map of the gardens is available from the information centre in the car park.

From the car park turn left following the 'Walks' sign to reach the Temple of Concord and Victory.

This was built by William Kent about 1746. The temple includes fluted Ionic columns and an inscription which refers to the victorious end of the Seven Years' War.

Turn left along the Grecian Valley, also designed by William Kent.

This valley was originally intended to be a lake, but the designers had difficulty in making the water stay put. At the far end of the valley is the Fane of Pastoral Poetry, with a view across to an obelisk built in 1759 to mark the death of General Wolfe in the battle for Quebec.

(A) Follow the main path (marked by green arrows) to the Cobham Monument, erected as a belvedere in 1747 by Lord Cobham. Follow the main path round to the Queen's Temple, designed by Gibbs in the 1740s, later altered by Borra. From here, there is a view across to the Gothic Temple, visited later.

At a cross-paths, continue straight on along the Elysian Fields, laid out by William Kent in the 1730s.

Along this gentle valley are the Seasons Fountain, where the water flows out of a lion's mouth, and Shell Bridge, which acts as a dam between the upper and lower parts of the lake. It was originally covered in shells. The Cook Monument was erected in 1778 in memory of Captain Cook. It originally had a globe on top.

Finally, the Temple of British Worthies is reached.

It was built by William Kent in 1733, one of the first of Stowe's monuments. It is in semi-circle form with sixteen recesses, each containing a bust, made by Rysbrack in 1732–3. The worthies

Figure in the Temple of British Worthies, built in 1733, one of Stowe's first monuments

displayed there are Queen Elizabeth I, Shakespeare, Bacon, Milton, Hampden, Newton, Locke, William III (who is in Roman dress), King Alfred, the Black Prince, Gresham, Sir John Barnard, Drake, Raleigh, Inigo Jones and Pope. It is a superb monument of national pride and historical interest, complete with an accurate portrayal of period costume.

(B) At the end of the Elysian Fields turn left towards the Palladian Bridge.

This was also built early in the garden's history, and was designed by Palladio. Other examples of this style are at Wilton House, near Salisbury, and at Prior Park, Bath. The bridge has unfluted Ionic columns. On the hillside to your left is the Gothic Temple. This is one of the most dominant of the Stowe monuments. It was built around 1840, when the Gothic revival was in its infancy. It was designed in a triangle, with a pentagonal tower at each corner, being taller in one corner than the other two.

(C) To explore the Gothic Temple turn left at the Palladian Bridge. After crossing the Palladian Bridge, the walk passes the Temple of

Friendship, the front of which has four large Tuscan columns. From here there is a good view across the lake and Palladian Bridge to the Gothic Temple. Later, the Lake Pavillions are reached – designed by Vanburgh in 1719. From here is a superb view across the Octagon Lake to Stowe School – the best view on the whole walk.

At the second Lake Pavilion bear right past a 'No Horses' sign, then turn left along the lakeside path. Separating the Octagon Lake from the Eleven Acre Lake is the Cascade, a pretty dam built from rocks with a rough pointed arch. Turn right at a cross-paths, following the main path round the Eleven Acre Lake.

To the left is the Temple of Venus, a raised alcove with two Ionic columns. At the other end of the long avenue are the Boycott Pavillions. They were originally connected by an arch, crossing the approach road.

(D) However, our route turns right at a green arrow to follow a secluded lakeside path. At the other end of the lake, the path passes the Cascade again. Here, turn left, then right almost immediately. At a second T- junction, turn left **(E)**, then right again to arrive back at the Elysian Fields, returning along the other side of the valley.

Almost at once, the Grenville Column is reached. This is a rostral column, with a statue of heroic beauty holding out a scroll towards the British Worthies on the far side of the lake.

A short detour brings you to the church of the Assumption, hidden by trees. The church is all that remains of the village of Stowe, which was moved when the park was built. After passing the Grotto at the head of the Elysian Fields, the path passes the buildings of Stowe School en route back to the Temple of Concorde and Victory. From here is a good view along the length of the Grecian Valley, together with a vista across to the Cobham Monument, visited earlier on the walk.

The tea room is located behind the Temple of Concorde and Victory.

WALK 4 – WING

DISTANCE:	12km/8 miles
TIME:	3 hours
MAP:	OS Landranger 165, OS Explorer 181 and 192
START:	Wing church (Grid Ref 882226)
REFRESHMENTS:	Bull and Butcher, Aston Abbotts; Rose and Crown, Wingrave

A walk linking three villages, all on rolling hills in the Vale of Aylesbury, by a series of fieldpaths across pastoral farmland. Although the walk never rises more than 200ft (67m) above sea level, there are wide views all around, with the distant Chiltern escarpment as a backdrop.

START: The village of Wing. There is a small parking area for about five cars at the bend in the road by the churchyard. Otherwise on-street parking is available in the quiet Church Street (grid ref 882226). Wing is reached from Aylesbury by proceeding northeast on the A418. Buses from Aylesbury and Leighton Buzzard stop at Wing.

THE WALK: From the bend in Church Street turn left along the path passing to the left of the church.

The Anglo-Saxon church of All Saints is a rare survivor of Saxon architecture, with its seven-sided apse, crypt, nave and aisle. According to John Betjeman it is 'The finest Saxon Church in Britain'. At the entrance to the tower (which is now blocked by the organ), there are a couple of Saxon doorways high up in the wall, which may once have led to a gallery. The wooden roof is one of the finest in Buckinghamshire. The roof trusses contain carvings of angels, while the cross-beams contain carvings of saints, kings and grotesques. There are also several monuments to the Dormer family, who lived at Ascott House to the east of the village, now owned by the National Trust. It was originally a minster church, from where the monks went out to preach to

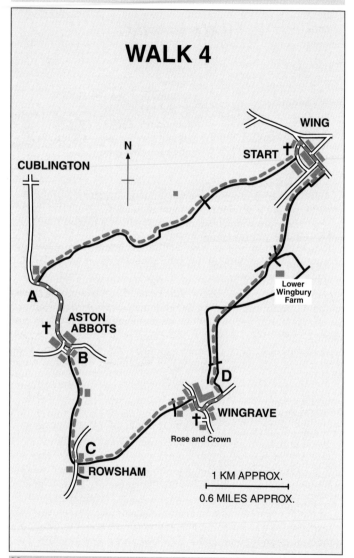

WALK 4

WING

START

CUBLINGTON

N

Lower
Wingbury
Farm

A

ASTON
ABBOTS

B

D

WINGRAVE

Rose and Crown

C

ROWSHAM

1 KM APPROX.

0.6 MILES APPROX.

the churchless villages around. As more churches were built the monks were replaced by the village priest.

At a kissing gate, continue straight on across the field to a stile ahead. Continue straight on across the next field (ignore two waymark arrows indicating paths going off to the right). Pass to the right of a hillock ahead to reach a stile in the opposite fence. Cross the foot-bridge and proceed to hedge gap ahead and on to a stile at the top of a rise. Continue along the right-hand side of the next field. Cross the next field via a wide grassy track, which continues along the right-hand edge of the next field. At the far side of the next field bear slightly left across the next field (path well defined). Cross straight on over a cross-paths at a waymark post.

To the right are some dilapadated buildings which once were living quarters/stores for RAF Wing, a wartime Bomber Command aerodrome opened in 1941 on land to the north. More recently this was a proposed site for London's third airport. Thankfully the Council and local residents convinced the government that the whole idea of building an airport in such a rural idyll was a non-starter.

Continue straight on at a second cross-paths. After crossing a foot-bridge on the far side of the field, turn left along the left-hand edge of the next field to a stile in the field corner. After crossing this stile turn right along the right-hand edge of the next field. Continue along the right-hand edge of a series of fields via stiles and yellow waymarks to reach a road. **(A)** Turn left along this road to reach the village of Aston Abbots.

The church of St James was restored by G.E. Street in 1865-6, but sadly the church is not usually open. The east window is in memory of Rear Admiral Sir James Clark Ross, who discovered the Magnetic Pole in 1831. He once lived in the Abbey, a large house on the western side of the village. Before the Dissolution it was owned by the Abbott of St. Albans as a country seat. During the Second World War, Dr Edward Benes, the former president of Czechoslovakia lived in exile here. The village shop is the oldest building in the village, dating back to 1640.

(B) Turn left along the road signposted to Wingrave. Turn right along a road opposite the Bull and Butcher, past the village shop. Turn

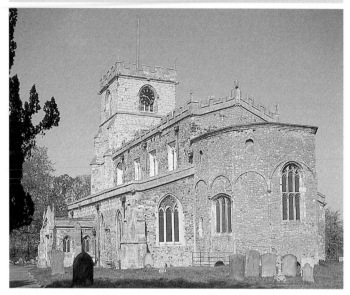

Wing church, a fine example of Saxon architecture

left along Brickstock (once believed to be a stacking place for locally made bricks). Go through the gate and cross the recreation ground to a stile, and continue on down the right-hand side of the next field. Ahead is a fine view across to the Chilterns. Pass to the right of a barn on the ridge-top, then continue along the left-hand side of a couple of fields linked by a kissing gate. Bear right to a gate, then proceed down across a large field, bearing left to a stile to the right of a house ahead. Bear left across a field to a stile in the far left-hand corner to come out onto the A418 at Rowsham, a collection of cottages.

(C) Turn right along the road for a few paces, then turn left along Brewhouse Lane. At the end cross over a stile after passing a couple of ponds and a forlorn disused chapel. Cross the field to a stile in the left-hand field corner. Continue along the left-hand edge of the next field. Cross over a footbridge and follow the path across the middle of the next field to a stile/footbridge near the left-hand corner. Cross the next field to a metal gate ahead, then continue on to a stile by the next gate. Continue along the left-hand edge of the next field to a stile in the field corner, and on up a track to reach Wingrave. Turn right at a T-junction past the church.

The church of SS. Peter and Paul is a Victorian-style building – an 1898 rebuild of the original Perpendicular (English Gothic style) church built in the 13th century. Compared with many village churches in Buckinghamshire, the interior is spacious. BBONT (Buckinghamshire, Berkshire and Oxfordshire Naturalists' Trust) have recognised the churchyard as a haven for wildlife. The village itself is very much a Rothschild village (see Introduction), but without a mansion. The village school and some cottages were built by the Rothschilds from 1876 onwards. There are some Rothschild cottages on the road leading to the village from the A418. The village is built on a hilltop between the Rothschild houses at Ascott and Mentmore.

To the east of the village is the Manor House. During the Second World War it was the headquarters of the exiled Czech government. For the Rose and Crown pub turn right just after the church. To continue the walk proceed straight on along Leighton Road, past the village pond on your right. **(D)** Turn left over a stile between fences just after the entrance to the Manor House. Continue straight on across paddocks via a series of stiles. Turn left along the left-hand edge of a large field. Where the hedge/field boundary bends left, continue straight on across the field to a line of trees ahead and proceed along by these trees (on your left). Later there is a hedge on your left. Wing is seen ahead.

Continue straight on over cross-paths. Cross over a footbridge and bear left across the next field. Cross over a track and further footbridge, then bear right across the next field to a hedge gap. Turn left past some young pine trees, then bear right across the next field (maintaining the same direction as before) towards Lower Wingbury Farm ahead.

On the far side of the field cross over a track and carry straight on along a grassy track. Bear right along a narrow path by a yellow waymark arrow alongside a ditch on your left. This path tends to get overgrown in the summer months. When the farm track is reached turn left, crossing a bridge over a ditch. Bear right across the next field (via a yellow waymark). The path drops to a footbridge, then continues across the next field, climbing gently.

Just before the A418 is reached, continue along the left-hand edge of the field, parallel to the road. Looking back from the top of the rise, there is a fine view back to Wingrave and the Chiltern escarpment beyond. Later the path bends right, then left again to run along the back of some houses. To the right are some fine views across to the Chiltern escarpment.

Turn left along a minor road to arrive back in Wing. Continue straight along the A418, then carry on along the High Street when the main road bends right. Turn left along Church Street back to the start. Wing has a selection of pubs and shops. The pump (close to the church) commemorates the marriage of the Prince of Wales to Princess Alexandra of Denmark on 10 March 1863.

WALK 5 – THE CLAYDONS

DISTANCE :	**11km/7 miles**
TIME:	**3 hours**
MAP:	**OS Landranger 165, OS Explorer 192**
START:	**By East Claydon church (Grid Ref 739256)**
REFRESHMENTS:	**Tea rooms, Claydon House**

A pleasant walk through the fieldpaths connecting three small villages, which, though they may be only a few miles from Aylesbury as the crow flies, are some of the most remote villages in Buckinghamshire, being accessible only by country lanes. The highlight of the walk is Claydon House, now owned by the National Trust. The walk passes close by the west front of the house.

START: East Claydon. There is a small parking area by the church (grid ref 739256), and further parking available at the west end of Botolph Claydon. The Claydons are signposted from Winslow on the A413 and reached from the A41 by Quainton. The church is at the eastern side of the village, reached by turning along Church Way, where the

View of Stowe School from across the Octagon Lake (Walk 3)

The Temple of British Worthies at Stowe Landscape Gardens (Walk 3)

The Palladian Bridge at Stowe Landscape Gardens (Walk 3)

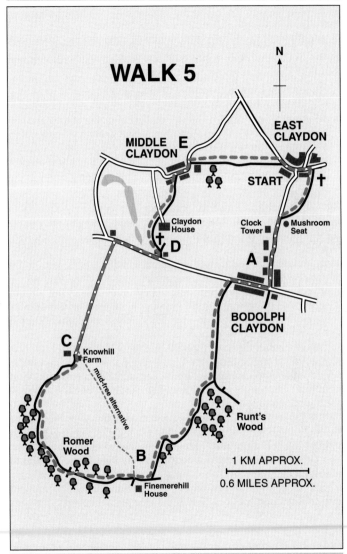

WALK 5

N

EAST CLAYDON

MIDDLE CLAYDON E

START

Claydon House

Clock Tower

Mushroom Seat

D

A

BODOLPH CLAYDON

C

Knowhill Farm

mud-free alternative

Runt's Wood

Romer Wood

B

Finemerehill House

1 KM APPROX.

0.6 MILES APPROX.

main road through the village swings north to Winslow. Buses from Winslow and Aylesbury connect with the Claydons.

THE WALK: Head southwest along a tarmac path between hedges past a 'Footpath Only – No Horses' sign. Later merge with road and continue south towards Botolph Claydon.

On the boundary between East Claydon and Botolph Claydon is a clock tower built in 1913. There is a clock face on each side of the tower – one for each village. On the other side of the road is a mushroom seat – a wooden bench built around a living oak tree with a thatched roof. Weir Cottage is typical of the cottages in the village, and is now a listed building. It is a traditional black and white cottage with a thatched roof built around 1700.

(A) Follow the main road round to the right. Turn left along a track by a public bridleway/circular walk sign. Further parking is available here. The wide verges alongside the track have been a nesting place for ground-nesting partridges. Where the track forks take the right fork, passing to the right of Runt's Wood. Like all the woods on the walk, Runt's Wood is part of the ancient Bernwood Forest. In the spring, the ground becomes a carpet of bluebells. Turn right at a T-junction, past a barn. Ahead is a superb view across the Vale of Aylesbury to Quainton Hill, Waddesdon with the Chiltern escarpment beyond. On a clear day, the Telecom tower at Stokenchurch can be seen.

(B) Once past the barn, the walk continues to Knowhill Farm past Romer Wood and Sheephouse Wood. This part of the route can be very muddy, especially after rain. For a mud-free alternative, turn right at a T-junction along a track through Greatsea Wood (where roe and fallow deer have been spotted).

For the main route, continue straight on over the fence, then along the right-hand side of the field, descending to a bridlegate. Pass through this bridlegate and continue along the woodland path. Romer and Greatsea Woods are now forestry plantations. These woods are managed for timber. The main trees are oak and pine, but there are also areas of red cedar and poplar. A forest ride going off to the right is for forestry purposes only and is not a public right of way. The path through the wood is very muddy. Follow the main path through the woods, ignoring all turnings off. At the end of the woods pass through a bridlegate and continue along the left-hand side of the field to Knowhill Farm. Turn left through a gate at the top of a rise passing between farm buildings.

(C) Continue straight on along the farm drive ignoring a track going off to the right. (the end of the mud-free alternative). Alongside the long drive is an avenue of poplars. Turn right along the road at the end of the drive. (D) By a public bridleway sign, turn left past the lodge to enter the grounds of Claydon House. Where the drive bends right, bear slightly left to a gate to pass left of All Saints Church, Middle Claydon and Claydon House.

Claydon House has been the seat of the Verney Family since 1620. In the Civil War, Sir Edmund Verney was the standard bearer for Charles I. He was killed in the Battle of Edgehill still gripping the royal standard. His hand had to be hacked off in order for the flag to be released from his grip. His ghost is said to appear at Claydon House whenever his family or country are threatened.

The present house dates from the 18th century, when it was rebuilt by Ralph, second Earl Verney in an over-ambitious plan to emulate Stowe and to further his political career. The park was landscaped, with a series of ornamental lakes being built to the west to look as natural as possible, and the house was redesigned and enlarged. The original design included a huge rotunda on the north side of the present west wing (from the dome it was claimed that the Welsh mountains could be seen) and an identical wing on the other side, which was one large ballroom. This building project, together with some bad investments, led to Lord Verney becoming bankrupt in 1784. Most of the fixtures and fittings were sold by his creditors. The rotunda and ballroom were demolished after his death in 1791 – the ballroom was not even completed. The most spectacular room in the house is the Chinese room, containing some extraordinary rococo decoration, built when the Chinese influence was at is height. Along with the North Hall, saloon and staircase, it is the sole survivor of Earl Verney's ambitious plans in the 18th century.

In the 19th century, Sir Harry Calvert (who had changed his name to Verney on inheriting Claydon) visited Java and Indonesia before becoming MP for Buckingham. He brought back some Indonesian musical instruments, which are now on display in Claydon House. In 1858 he married Frances Parthenope, the sister of Florence Nightingale. Florence was a regular visitor to Claydon and always stayed in the same room, which now bears her name. The museum contains a collection of items relating to Florence Nightingale, known as 'The Lady with the Lamp' when nursing in Scutari in the Crimean War. Later (with Sir Harry) she was involved in the design of the Royal Buckinghamshire Hospital in Aylesbury.

The church of All Saints stands on a hillock close to the south wing of the house in the middle of the garden. The graveyard was moved at the time of the second Earl Verney's ambitious building project (much to the horror of the villagers). Claydon House is now owned by the National Trust (although the Verney family still live in the south wing). The rooms in the west wing are open to the public from April to October from Saturday to Wednesday (although the exact opening times may vary from year to year). The house is well worth a visit. There is also a tea room open on the same days as the house. Tea is served in one of the outbuildings.

On the far side of the house turn right at a bridlegate to reach the main drive, then bear right to a bridlegate on the top of the rise in front of a tree. Continue along the left-hand side of the field to a bridlegate leading out to a road in the village of Middle Claydon (by a post box). **(E)** Turn right along this road. Turn right over a stile by a public footpath sign (hedge on left) just after a cemetery (the displaced All Saints' churchyard?). After crossing a further stile, continue along the right-hand edge of a series of fields, climbing gently. When the hedge bends right at the top of the rise continue straight on across the field to a couple of gates, just to the right of a barn ahead. The path is not always clearly marked, but this is a public right of way used by the villagers. Continue along the left-hand side of the next field. Continue across the middle of the next field to a gate, passing a small pond on the left, to return to East Claydon. Turn right along the road. At a T-junction turn left (towards Winslow). Where the road bends left continue straight on along Church Way. Turn right along a cul-de-sac back to the church and the start of the walk.

WALK 6 – QUAINTON

DISTANCE:	**12km/7½ miles**
TIME:	**3 hours**
MAP:	**OS Landranger 165, OS Explorer 192**
START:	**By East Claydon church (Grid Ref 739256)**
REFRESHMENTS:	**George and Dragon, Quainton**

Starting from East Claydon, this walk is dominated by Quainton Hill, one of the highest points in the Vale of Aylesbury. After visiting the pretty village of Quainton with its restored windmill the walker climbs up to the summit of Quainton Hill, the effort being rewarded with fine views across the Vale of Aylesbury.

START: East Claydon. There is limited parking in the cul-de-sac by the church (grid ref 739256). The Claydons are signposted from Winslow on the A413, and are reached via Quainton from the A41. The church, on the eastern side of the village, is reached by turning along Church Way, where the main road through the village swings north towards Winslow. Buses from Winslow and Aylesbury connect with the Claydons, and also stop in Quainton, where further parking is available

THE WALK: From East Claydon church head southwest along a tarmac path between hedges, past a 'Footpath Only – No Horses' sign. Later continue along the road to Botolph Claydon, past the Mushroom Seat (a bench built around a living oak tree with a thatched roof), the clock tower (built in 1913 to mark the boundary between East Claydon and Botolph Claydon) and the public library (built and stocked by the Verneys, who lived at nearby Claydon House).

   (A) Where the road bends right (and the road towards Quainton goes off to the left), continue straight on along a farm drive past a phone box and a large duckpond. At a gate continue straight on across the field ahead in the direction of the left-hand waymark arrow to a stile in the opposite fence. Pass to the right of a large compost

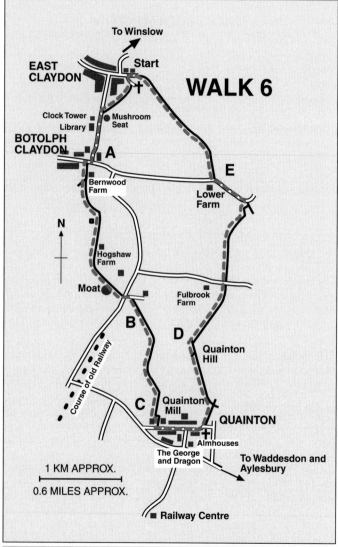

To Winslow

EAST CLAYDON

Start

WALK 6

Clock Tower
Library
Mushroom Seat

BOTOLPH CLAYDON

A

E

Bernwood Farm

Lower Farm

N

Hogshaw Farm

Moat

Fulbrook Farm

Course of old Railway

B

D

Quainton Hill

C

Quainton Mill

QUAINTON

Almhouses

The George and Dragon

To Waddesdon and Aylesbury

1 KM APPROX.

0.6 MILES APPROX.

Railway Centre

mound. The path continues across the next field to a gate. Continue across the next field in the direction of a waymark arrow (the path is well defined across these fields) to a gate in the opposite corner.

Among the crops planted in these fields is oil seed rape, which blooms in the spring with bright yellow flowers. On a wide view across farmland in areas like the Vale of Aylesbury a large field of oil seed rape in full bloom is striking – the patches of yellow being in complete contrast to the various shades of green around.

After crossing a track bear right to a gate leading to a grassy track. Again the path is well defined. Continue across the next field to a hedge gap and stile. Cross the next field to a stile by a pond in the opposite far corner. Pass to the right of a pylon to reach a waymark post by the pond. Bear left across the next field to a stile, crossing the remains of a moat, and on to a further stile by a gate. Cross over the road and proceed along the drive to Hill Cottage Farm.

At this point the walk crosses the former route of the Metropolitan Railway which extended across the Vale to Brill and Verney Junction until the line was closed to passengers in 1936 (although it was used by goods trains until the 1960s). A mile south of Quainton, Quainton station is now a railway museum. Thankfully 'Metroland', with its shops and rows of near identical semi-detached houses, never reached this far – the distance and (even in the 1930s) fares made commuting into London unattractive. Today you would need to take out a second mortgage for an annual season from Quainton to Baker Street!

(B) Turn right over a stile in the fence and bear left across the field (towards the corner of a wood ahead between a couple of ponds) to a stile by a gate. Although the course of the path across the fields to Quainton is not obvious, the route is well waymarked. Bear right across the next field to a stile/waymark post near the opposite corner and continue across the next field to a stile by a gate. Continue along the right-hand edge of the next three fields. In the third field, bear left to a metal gate where the hedge bears left (after passing stile on your right). After passing through gate, cross over stile to reach a stile in the opposite hedge. Continue along a path between hedges. Turn left at a T-junction to reach the village of Quainton. **(C)** Turn left along the road along the top of the village.

Quainton is dominated by a tower mill. The windmill was built in 1830 from hand-made bricks. The original owner was James Anstiss, and the mill is still in the ownership of the same family. In recent years the windmill has been restored, with the sails now added. At the top of the village green is a stone block and shaft from a 14th-century cross. Funerals from neighbouring farms waited here for the rector to lead them to the church. At the other end of the village green is the excellent George and Dragon pub. It has a wide selection of well-priced food and is an ideal stop for a break. The historian (and doctor for nearby Whitchurch) George Lipscombe lived at Magpie Cottage on the corner of the village green. He wrote a four-volume 'History of the Antiquities of the County of Buckingham'. He is commemorated by a tablet in the church.

The almshouses next to the church were built by Richard Winwood in the 1680s in a pre-classical style. There is a monument to him and his wife in the church. Other monuments in the church include two to the Dormers.

Follow the road along the top of the village past the almshouses and church. Turn left over a stile just after the church. Cross the field to a stile and continue straight on across the next field to a public bridleway sign at the hedge corner. Turn left along a track (the Swan's Way). Follow the track up to the radio mast on the summit of Quainton Hill.

There are superb views across the Vale of Aylesbury from Quainton Hill. Looking south beyond the village, Waddesdon Hill is clearly seen. When Baron de Rothschild had Waddesdon Manor (see Walk 7) built on the ridge, the top was flattened and a railway was built from Quainton Station to carry the stone for the house and trees for the park. Beyond, the Chiltern escarpment is visible, and to the north the Shropshire hills can apparently be seen on a clear day.

Follow the track across two fields on the top of the ridge. **(D)** At the end of the second field pass through the gate and bear right, descending down the field between a mound (on your left) and some trees (on your right) to reach a bridlegate to the right of a barn at the foot of the hill. Continue across the next field, then bear right to a stile and public footpath sign to the right of a telegraph pole ahead. Cross over a track and continue in the direction of a public footpath/North Bucks Way sign to a stile in the fence opposite. The North Bucks Way crosses the fields via a series of stiles. Keep on going in the same direction.

After crossing a footbridge and stile, bear right across the next field to a footbridge (in front of a hill ahead, to the left of a pylon). On the hilltop ahead is the country town of Winslow. Follow the path between hedge and fence, over a footbridge, and left along a track to reach a road. **(E)** Turn left along this road. After about 500 yards turn right across a large traingular field (by a North Bucks Way sign) to a gate in the far corner. Continue along the right-hand edge of the next field. On the ridge-top ahead is East Claydon church, with Botolph Claydon to the left. Later the path follows the left-hand edge of the third field for the final (gentle) climb. Later merge with track. Once back in East Claydon, turn left along a cul-de sac (past the church notice board) back to the start.

The church is unremarkable as a result of a 19th-century restoration. Nearby is the White House. Here Edmund Verney and his wife, Mary Abell, lived after their marriage in 1662. Behind the mixed brick and stone walls are some formal gardens. The house is not open to the public.

WALK 7 – WADDESDON

DISTANCE:	**10km/6 miles**
TIME:	**2 hours 30 mins**
MAP :	**OS Landranger 165, OS Explorer 181**
START:	**Waddesdon High Street, near the Five Arrows Hotel (Grid Ref 740169)**
REFRESHMENTS:	**White Swan, Westcott; Five Arrows, Waddesdon**

A gentle walk dominated by the French chateaux-inspired Waddesdon Manor. There is only one easy climb through the

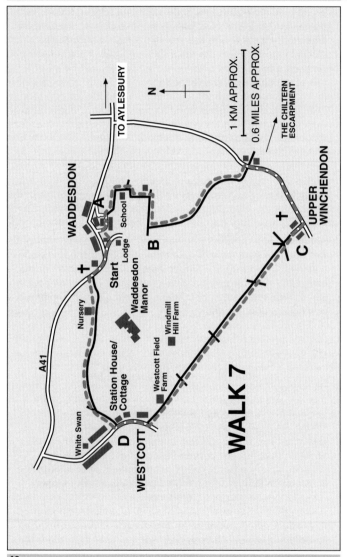

WALK 7

grounds of Waddesdon Manor, which rewards the walker with a view across the Thame Valley to the Chiltern escarpment, together with the prospect of the manor which inspired a 'Country Life' writer to comment 'Its lofty tournalles and skyward elaborations might well be lifted above the swelling foliage of thick woods in Touraine'.

START: The linear village of Waddesdon, 6 miles west of Aylesbury on the A41. There is a wide parking area alongside the A41 near the Five Arrows Hotel and the war memorial at the start of the walk. A Red Rover bus service connects Waddesdon with Aylesbury.

THE WALK: From the Five Arrows Hotel and the war memorial turn left along the drive to Waddesdon Manor. Turn left along a path opposite a lodge house (not signposted), just before the gates leading into Waddesdon Manor Park are reached. Where the path forks, fork left, then turn right along a road. **(A)** Bear right along School Lane, then bear left along a path passing to the left of the school. Where the tarmac path turns left, keep straight on, following the perimeter of the school playing fields. Continue straight on where the North Bucks Way goes off to the left. Turn left over a stile through some pines to reach a further stile, then continue along the left-hand edge of the next field, passing a cottage to reach one of the drives across Waddesdon Manor Park.

Turn right along this drive **(B)**, then turn left through a gate at the top of the rise. Follow this track across the park, gently rising to a road along the ridge-top.

Just before reaching the road is a fine view across to Waddesdon Manor rising from the tree tops. The manor was built by Baron Ferdinand de Rothschild in the 1870s on the hill above the village. The top of the hill had to be levelled off to build the manor, together with the landscaped gardens. The manor is a touch of France in the pastoral Buckinghamshire landscape. The French theme is carried over to the interior, with French design panelling, furniture, carpets and porcelain. The manor also contains a collection of 18th-century portraits by Gainsborough and Reynolds, together with some 17th-century Dutch masters. The landscaped gardens are equally impressive, and include a formal parterre and a rococo-style aviary containing some exotic birds. The house and grounds are now owned by the National Trust and are open from Easter to October from Thursday to Sunday and Bank Holiday Monday (plus Wednesday in July and August), although the exact details may change from year to year (tel. 01296 651226 for details).

Turn right along the road (it is not too busy). To the left is a wide view across the Thame Valley to the Chiltern escarpment. **(C)** After about ¾ mile, turn right down the drive to Decoy Farm. Continue down a concrete path following a public bridleway waymark, then continue down the right-hand edge of two fields. Cross the third field to a gate. In the next field, bear left following a circular walk waymark to a gate in the far corner. Continue along the right-hand edge of the next two fields, ignoring a crossing track. Cross the next field in the direction of a blue waymark. Continue along the right-hand edge of the next field, then on along a track, passing to the left of a farm (fence on your right) to reach a road on the outskirts of the village of Westcott. Turn right along this road.

Westcott is a village in the shadow of Waddesdon Manor, although it boasts a fine pub, the White Swan, which has a good selection of beers and reasonably priced food – ideal for a break before the final stretch back to Waddesdon. About ¼ mile along the road are Station House and Station Cottage. These cottages were formerly Westcott station, a halt on the Brill Tramway, built in 1871 to transport coal and produce around the Duke of Buckingham's estate. It was acquired by the Metropolitan Railway in 1899. By all accounts travel on the Brill line was a leisurely affair, with the train making frequent stops to let passengers on and off, and the drivers not averse to stopping the train so that they could go off into the fields to have a tea (or beer) break! The line was closed in 1935, two years after passing into the owner-ship of London Transport. (Today the railway stops at Aylesbury.)

(D) Turn right over a stile by a public footpath sign just after Station House. (For the White Swan pub, continue straight on along the road for about ¼ mile). Cross the field to a stile in the opposite fence. Ignore the track continuing straight on. Cross over the stile and turn half-right across the field to a stile in the opposite fence (heading roughly due east). The path continues across the next field to reach a track. To the left is a view across the Vale of Aylesbury towards Quainton, with Quainton Hill as a backdrop.

Continue along this track, which runs along the base of Lodge Hill (with Waddesdon Manor hidden behind the trees). After passing the former kitchen gardens and stables of Waddesdon Manor, which are now a nursery, the track becomes a metalled lane. Turn right along the A41 back to the start. Waddesdon Manor is well worth a visit after the walk. It has a tea room as well! The end of the walk passes through the old part of Waddesdon, of which only St. Michael's church and the Bell pub remain.

WALK 8 – BRILL

DISTANCE :	**7km/4½ miles**
TIME:	**2 hours**
MAP:	**OS Landranger 165, OS Explorer 180**
START:	**Brill, near the church and village green (Grid Ref 656138)**
REFRESHEMENTS:	**Pheasant pub, Brill**

A short but varied walk starting from Brill, a hilltop village near the Oxfordshire border. The walk includes a forest, a view across to Wotton House, and a nature reserve before the climb back to Brill, with its landmark windmill (and the excellent Pheasant pub!).

START: Brill village is reached by a minor road climbing the hill from the B4011, northwest of Long Crendon (grid ref 656138). The village is signposted from Long Crendon (2 miles north of Thame). There is a small car park by the windmill (and the Pheasant pub) and several places for on-street parking near the church. As for public transport – forget it! Although there is a sparse bus service linking Brill with Aylesbury and Oxford, it is not frequent enough to be relied upon for reaching the walk and getting home again in one day. The walk starts near the village green and All Saints church.

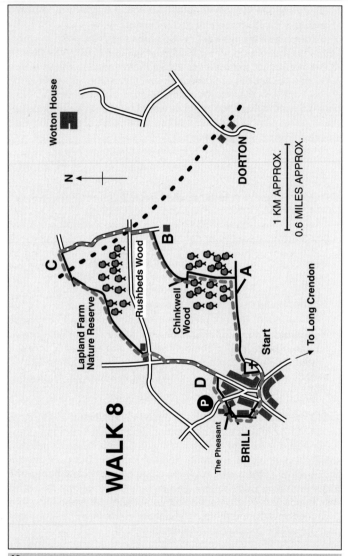

WALK 8

Wotton House

N

Lapland Farm
Nature Reserve

Rushbeds Wood

Chinkwell
Wood

C

B

A

DORTON

1 KM APPROX.
0.6 MILES APPROX.

The Pheasant

P D

BRILL

Start

To Long Crendon

All Saints church was rebuilt in 1888, when it was much enlarged, although traces of the Norman doorways and chancel remain. The roof was built in the 17th century. The font cover was made by Canon Vernon Staley, in about 1918–20. The village green is set away from the church. Around the green are a number of houses built with vitreous brick with a red brick dressing – a Brill characteristic!

THE WALK: Take the track to the left of the church, then follow the left-hand edge of the recreation ground. Turn right along a tarmac path to reach a T-junction in the middle of a housing estate. Turn left here, then continue along a track by a public footpath sign. Pass through a gate and continue straight on in the direction of a waymark arrow. Ahead is a fine view across the Vale of Aylesbury. Cross over the next stile and bear left to follow the outside edge of Chinkwell Wood.

(A) Near the bottom of the slope, turn left over a stile and across a footbridge to enter the woods. (It is easy to miss!) Follow this path along a ride straight on across the wood heedless of all turnings off (it is the only public right of way through the wood). On the far side turn left over a stile along a path between fences.

Turn right along a track, then bear left over a stile in the direction of a yellow waymark arrow (hedge on your right). **(B)** Later turn left along a drive to reach a minor road. Turn right along this road, crossing over the railway, then turn left. Later there is a fine vista across to Wotton House.

Wotton House was built for Richard Grenville in the early 18th century, complete with a landscape garden (a mini Stowe). The house was rebuilt after a fire in 1820. After a second fire in 1929 it stood derelict until the 1950s, when it was rebuilt and converted into flats. The house and gardens are not open to the public, and many of the garden monuments have now been removed.

(C) Where the road bends right, turn left along a track by a public bridleway sign. After crossing the railway again, bear left through a kissing gate to enter Lapland Farm Nature Reserve. Cross a worn path across the meadow to the woods ahead.

Lapland Farm Nature Reserve includes a natural meadow, full of wild flowers. It is one of the last remaining natural meadows in Buckinghamshire. A large variety of flowers grow here, including Heath-Dogs Violet. This is only one of three sites in Buckinghamshire where this flower is found. Nearby Rushbeds Wood contains a number of woodland walks. A booklet describing the walks is available from the nursery opposite.

On the far side turn right through a pair of gates and continue along the outside edge of the wood (Rushbeds Wood). At the end of the woods continue along the left-hand edge of a series of fields. Later, Brill village and windmill are seen ahead.

On reaching a road continue straight on along the road opposite (signposted to Brill), climbing back up to the village. **(D)** Turn right through a kissing gate at the top of Tram Hill (just before the 30mph limit sign). Follow this path across the field, passing to the left of a couple of hornbeam trees, before bearing left to a fence. After passing between some more trees you come out opposite the windmill and Pheasant pub.

The windmill was built in 1688 and is Brill's most famous land-mark. The surrounding common contains several pock marks – a result of clay workings. Until the 19th century bricks, tiles and pots were made in the village potteries. Today, these pock marks are grassed over, making a great play area for children. The common itself provides wide views and is a popular beauty spot for the locals. To the north was the terminus of the Brill branch of the Metropolitan Railway, which was closed in 1935.

The Pheasant pub is recommended for a break before the final stretch of the walk. As well as a garden there is a patio which overlooks the common and windmill. There is a wide selection of drinks and food available.

Continue straight on down South Hills (between the pub and windmill). At the end of the tarmac turn left up a track. Just before the end of the track, turn left over a stile (fence on your right). Continue straight on along the alleyway. Ignore a path coming in from the left. On reaching a road turn left to reach the village green, then turn right to return to the church (and the parked car).

WALK 9 – THAME VALLEY

DISTANCE :	13km/8 miles
TIME:	3 hours
MAP :	OS Landranger 165, OS Explorer 181
START :	Nether Winchendon (Grid Ref 734123)
REFRESHMENTS:	The Crown, Cuddington; Seven Stars, Dinton

A gentle walk with no steep climbs (save it for a hot day) across the fields to Dinton and the ruined folly, Dinton Castle, returning back along the Thame Valley.

START: The hamlet of Nether Winchendon (grid ref 734123). It is reached from Aylesbury by proceeding west along the A41, then turning left at a cross-roads 1 mile west of Waddesdon. Nether Winchendon is reached by turning left down a narrow lane after about 3 miles. Nether Winchendon is not accessible by public transport, but there is an hourly bus service from Aylesbury to Cuddington (Monday to Saturday), from where the walk can be picked up. Park in Nether Winchendon near the church.

THE WALK: Head west along the lane through the hamlet, passing the church on the right.

Nether Winchendon is a pretty hamlet set behind the water meadows of the Thame. At the centre of the village is the church of St. Nicholas. The exterior was rebuilt in 1891, but the interior is largely original, with box-pews and a 15th-century stained-glass window. The north wall of the nave contains boards with the Lord's Prayer, Ten Commandments and the Nicene Creed.

(A) Turn left along a path opposite a telephone box. Proceed between fences along a metalled path across the water meadows, climbing gently to the village of Cuddington.

As the village is approached, the church (also St. Nicholas) is seen. Cuddington is a pretty village made up of narrow lanes

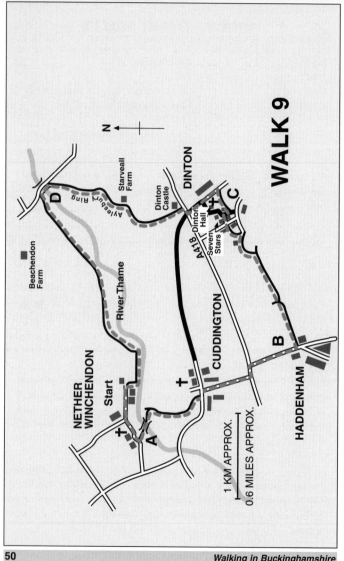

WALK 9

NETHER WINCHENDON

Start

A

River Thame

Beachendon Farm

D

Aylesbury Ring

Starveall Farm

DINTON

Dinton Castle

Dinton Hall

Seven Stars

C

A418

CUDDINGTON

B

HADDENHAM

N

1 KM APPROX.
0.6 MILES APPROX.

with little greens and witchert walls (the local building style). In his later years, Tom Stephenson lived in the village. Tom was one of Britain's most famous ramblers, who was the National Secretary of the Ramblers' Association. His greatest achievement was pioneering the Pennine Way, Britain's first long-distance foot- path, running for 250 miles along the backbone of the country.

In the village, turn left along the road, then turn right along the road signposted to Haddenham (opposite the Crown pub). When the main A418 road is reached turn left, then right along Churchway to reach the outskirts of Haddenham. **(B)** Fork left along Stanbridge Road, then immediately left along a track by a public bridleway sign. On the right is a general store where supplies can be bought.

Further on, this track gets overgrown in the summer, but is still passable. Where the track bends left, continue straight on over a stile. Bear right across the field in the direction of a waymark arrow to a stile and continue along the right-hand edge of the next field. Cross over two stiles in the field corner and continue along the right-hand edge of the next three fields. After crossing the next stile, bear left to a further stile in the fourth field (ahead is the village of Dinton). Continue in the same direction to the field edge, then bear right across the field to a stile by a gate (and public footpath sign).

Turn left up a drive and right over a stile. Cross the field in the direction of the top waymark arrow (straight on, not bearing left). Head towards a stile in the opposite corner. Continue along the right- hand edge of the next field and on along by fence (on your left) via a path between gardens to come out at a lane, opposite the Seven Stars pub. This is a good place for a break – at about the halfway mark.

Dinton is a rather scattered village, the church and Dinton Hall (see below) being located to the east, away from the village, which has a selection of pretty cottages. The church is not usually open.

Cross over the road and go down the lane opposite, past the pub. **(C)** Turn right along a lane (now metalled) at the bottom of the slope, then left at a T-junction. Where this lane bends right, bear left onto a path between fences, which then continues along the left-hand edge of two fields via kissing gates to reach another road. To the right there is a view across to the Chiltern escarpment, while Dinton Hall is seen to the left.

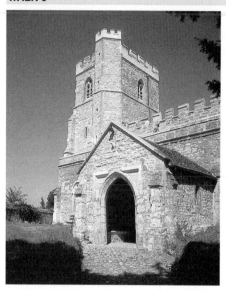

Dinton church, adjacent to Dinton Hall at the eastern end of the village

Dinton Hall is large, with many gables and chimneys, but there is little known about the building of the place. It looks to be 14th century in origin, but other parts appear to date from the 16th century, and it has 17th-century gate posts.

Turn left along the road, climbing gently to the church.

The church of St. Peter and St. Paul has an elaborate Norman doorway, while the tower is Perpendicular (English Gothic style, c.1350–1530). The nave is mainly 13th century. The chancel was extended in 1868.

Ignore a turning off to the left (this leads back to the village) and continue climbing gently up to the main A418 road. Here turn right (there is a pavement), then left over a stile, passing the ruins of Dinton Castle.

Dinton Castle was built by Sir John Vanhatten in 1769, when he lived at Dinton Hall. It was built as a folly (or ruin) on a Saxon burial mound in a spinney.

The next section of the walk follows part of the Aylesbury Ring, a 30-mile circular path which passes across pastoral farmland while only being a few miles from Aylesbury, the largest town (and administrative centre) of Buckinghamshire.

Continue along the right-hand edge of the field, then turn right over a stile by an Aylesbury Ring waymark post. Bear left across the next field, then turn right, following the left-hand edge of the field. Turn left over a footbridge in the field corner and turn right along the field edge. Pass through a hedge gap, and bear left across the next field.

Turn right along a track towards Starveall Farm ahead. Just before the farm turn left through a hedge gap (by waymark post) and continue along the right-hand edge of the next field. After crossing a footbridge, bear right across the next field to a stile. Bear left across a further field to a stile, then continue across the next field in the same direction to a stile, leading out to a lane. Turn left along this lane.

The walk now passes through the Eythorpe Estate, an area of parkland built by the Rothschilds. By the bridge is a waterfall, which was the site of a watermill before the mill site was drained and the River Thame raised to form an ornamental lake. Eythorpe Park was owned by Alice de Rothschild, and was one of the 19th-century houses built by the family in the Vale of Aylesbury.

(D) Just after the cattle grid bear left along a grassy path between a hedge and fence (the Thame Valley Walk). Cross over a stile, keeping to the right of the trees. At the end of the trees, where the track bends left, bear right across the middle of the field. BEWARE: there isn't a waymark post here.

Continue straight on across the third field to a stile in front of a tall tree ahead. After crossing a footbridge, bear left across the next field, passing to the left of the tree ahead.

At the next footbridge/stile, continue straight on across the next field, bearing left to a stile in the opposite fence. Continue along the left-hand edge of the next two fields. In the second field turn left over a stile, and cross the field to a hedge gap. Continue along a track between fences.

At the end of the track, turn right along the right-hand edge of the next field, later turning right towards a barn. Turn left along a track, passing to the right of this barn. Later, this track becomes metalled, and leads back to the start.

At the end of the walk, Nether Winchendon House is passed. It has been in the Bernard family since the 15th century. The house is largely Tudor, although it was Gothicized in 1780. It was restored, and the gardens were replanted, in 1958.

WALK 10 – BLEDLOW

DISTANCE :	**7km/4½ miles**
TIME:	**2 hours**
MAP:	**OS Landranger 165, OS Explorer 181**
START:	**Lay-by on the B4009 near Longwick (Grid Ref 788039)**
REFRESHMENTS:	**The Lions of Bledlow**

A mainly level walk across fieldpaths in the Vale of Aylesbury at the head of the Risborough Gap. Some of the paths are little used and tend to be overgrown in summer. However, these paths are not difficult to follow, and are all public rights of way.

START: A long lay-by on the B4009 near Longwick (grid ref 788039), a linear village consisting of modern properties. The lay-by is reached from Princes Risborough by heading northwest from the town on the A4129, then turning left along the B4009. The lay-by is just a few yards southwest of the B4444/B4009 junction.

THE WALK: Turn right along the B4009 from the lay-by (heading southwest). After passing underneath the railway, turn left along a track. After crossing a single-track railway, continue straight on along a path between fields (later passing some trees on your left). Later the path merges with a drive. Turn right along this drive to reach the hamlet of Horsenden.

Horsenden was once on the main route to Oxford. The church consists of a 15th-century chancel, which was once part of the older, larger medieval church which fell into disrepair. The church is usually locked. The tower was constructed in 1765 from the stones of the ruined nave. Horsenden Manor was built on the site of an older building in 1810.

(A) Where the track turns left (opposite the church), turn right over a stile (by public footpath sign) and continue on along the left-hand edge of a field. Cross the next field to a stile in the opposite fence. Continue straight on between fields and on along the right-

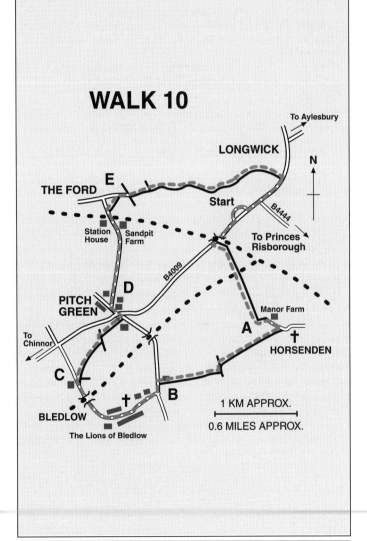

WALK 10

To Aylesbury

LONGWICK

N

THE FORD

E

Start

B4444

To Princes
Risborough

Station
House

Sandpit
Farm

B4009

D

PITCH
GREEN

Manor Farm

To
Chinnor

A

† HORSENDEN

C

B

1 KM APPROX.

0.6 MILES APPROX.

BLEDLOW

The Lions of Bledlow

hand edge of the next field. Turn left at a T-junction (in a line of trees).

Turn right over a stile and continue along the left-hand edge of two fields. To the right is a fine view across the Vale of Aylesbury. Follow the drive out to reach a road. Alongside this drive is a selection of old ploughs.

(B) Turn left along this road, then turn right along Church End, the main road through the village of Bledlow.

Bledlow is a pretty H-shaped village at the foot of the Chilterns. Next to the church is the Lyde Garden – a wooded ravine cut by a clear spring. The garden was created by Lord Carrington, who lives at the manor house. At one time there were watercress beds in the stream. There is a small pagoda in the middle of the stream at the base of the gorge.

Holy Trinity church was built in the 12th century. The windows in the southeastern wall of the nave and chancel were enlarged in the 14th century. The clock is set off-centre on the tower. Inside, the pews have been replaced with chairs, adapting the building to modern worship.

The village contains some pretty cottages made of timber and herringbone brickwork. The Lions of Bledlow is a fine pub at the western end of the village (in the shadow of the Chilterns) which is popular with walkers.

Follow the road round to the right, past the Lions pub. **(C)** After passing underneath the railway, turn right along a path between fences (opposite Westfield Farm). Ignore a stile just after leaving the road and continue alongside a stream. At a stile the path continues along the right-hand edge of a field (with the stream still on your right). After crossing a stile the path continues alongside the stream. This path is overgrown in summer, but not difficult to follow.

Turn right through a kissing gate and cross the field to a stile in the opposite fence by a hedge gap. Continue along the left-hand edge of the next field, passing to the left of a cottage to reach a road.

(D) Turn left along this road. Cross the B4009 and continue straight on along Sandpit Lane. Ignore a road going off to the left (Chapel Lane). After crossing the railway line turn right over a stile. Cross this field diagonally to a footbridge leading to a lane. Turn right along this lane, which later becomes a track.

At the point where Sandpit Lane crosses the single-track railway is the former Bledlow station – now converted to a house. This railway originally linked Princes Risborough to London and Oxford. The line was closed between Oxford and Thame in 1967, after passenger services were suspended in 1963. This part of the railway now carries oil deliveries from Kent and Essex to Thame.

(**E**) Where the track turns left, continue straight on along the right-hand edge of a field (following a waymark arrow), by a stream. Bear right through a hedge gap in the field corner. Bear right across the next field, then left along the field edge.

In the field corner, turn right through (a rather stiff) gate. Pass along the left-hand edge of the field, then continue across the field to the opposite corner (bear left). This path is little used, but passable.

Turn left through a gate, across the next field. Later the path runs alongside another stream. Bear left across the field, past a double telegraph pole to a rickety stile. Turn right along the B4009 back to the start.

WALK 11 – GREAT KIMBLE

DISTANCE:	**8km/5 miles**
TIME:	**2 hours**
MAP :	**OS Landranger 165, OS Explorer 181**
START:	**Lay-by on the A4010 at Great Kimble (Grid Ref 825059)**
REFRESHMENTS:	**Three Crowns, Askett; Bernard Arms, Great Kimble**

A level walk across the fieldpaths of the Vale of Aylesbury, with one of the most beautiful parts of the Chiltern escarpment as a backdrop.

START: A lay-by on the A4010 at Great Kimble (grid ref 825059). The lay-by is in a dip, just south of the church of St. Nicholas and the

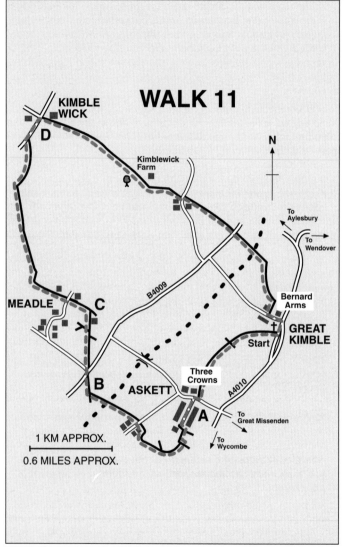

WALK 11

Bernard Arms pub. The A4010 is the main road linking Princes Risborough with Aylesbury. Bus 323/324 stops at Great Kimble.

THE WALK: From the northern end of the lay-by, cross the road and pass through a kissing gate, following a North Bucks Way waymark arrow. The path follows the right-hand edge of the field (bank on your right) to reach a stile by a telegraph pole. Continue across the next field to a stile. Cross over a drive and bear right across the next field to a stile in the field corner.

Continue along the left-hand edge of the next field (fence on your left). Continue with a line of trees on your left and on along the left-hand edge of the next field to reach Askett.

Askett is a village with no obvious centre, although it contains a fine pub, the Three Crowns, and some attractive cottages.

(A) Turn left along the road, past the Three Crowns pub, then left along Askett Lane. At the end of the lane turn left along a path between fences.

Turn right along by a wall (on your right). Continue across a series of paddocks, linked by a series of stiles. Turn right over a stile (with a dog gate) and go along a path between fences. Ignore a stile leading into a paddock. Bear right, following a fence on your left. After crossing a road, continue along the left -hand edge of the field opposite to reach the railway.

After crossing the railway, continue along the left-hand edge of the next field. Cross the next stile and continue (fence now on your right). **(B)** From the stile in the field corner bear right across a large field to a stile in the field corner.

Turn right along this road (the B4009), then bear left as if to go along the road signposted to Meadle. Continue straight on over a stile by a public footpath sign.

The walk now bypasses Meadle by a series of public footpaths. Meadle is a hamlet made up of brick-and-tile and white paint and thatched cottages. The painter John Nash wrote the first 'Shell Guide to Buckinghamshire' here in 1936.

Bear left, passing to the left of a nursery to reach a stile in the opposite fence. Continue straight on across the next field to reach a footbridge. **(C)** Pass along the right-hand edge of the meadow. Cross over a lane and continue straight on over a stile in the opposite hedge.

Bear slightly left across a large field to a stile in the opposite fence, and continue along the left-hand edge of the next field. When the far side of this field is reached turn right, then left over a stile in the hedge.

Bear right across the next field to a gate in the field corner, then continue across the next field in the same direction. Cross the next field to the opposite corner. The route of the footpath is faintly traced across the grass. After crossing a footbridge turn right along the right-hand edge of the next field. Pass through a gate and bear left across the next field to a stile in the opposite corner to reach a lane in Kimble Wick.

(D) Turn right along this lane. At a cross-roads turn right along a track (the North Bucks Way). Pass to the right of some farm buildings. Continue along the left-hand edge of the next three fields. In the fourth field, pass to the left of a spinney (with a pond in the middle). Cross over a stile and bear left across the field to a stile leading to the farm drive. Turn right along this drive (the Aylesbury Ring).

When a lane is reached, turn left then right over a stile (following an Aylesbury Ring waymark). Follow the right-hand edge of the field. Where the hedge turns right continue straight on.

Cross over a road and continue along a path between trees opposite. After crossing the railway, continue straight on along the left-hand edge of three fields to arrive back at Great Kimble (by the village school).

Great Kimble is claimed to be a corruption of 'Cymbeline' – a British king in Roman times. On the escarpment behind the walk is Cymbeline's Mount, an Iron Age hill fort. This, along with the Chiltern escarpment, is visible along the final part of the walk on the Aylesbury Ring. The parish of Great Kimble is a combination of two 'Chiltern Strip' parishes. These go back to Saxon times. The parishes were long and narrow at right angles to the hills. Thus, each parish encompassed different types of land, providing flint (for building) up in the hills, as well as woodland, arable land, fresh water from the spring at the foot of the hills and pasture land in the Vale of Aylesbury.

The 13th/14th-century church at Great Kimble was restored in Victorian times (1876–81). The altar is at the northern end and the tower is at the southern end of the building because the church is built on a north–south axis instead of the usual east–west axis.

In 1635, John Hampden and various other men of the parish refused to pay Ship Money, an additional tax imposed by Charles I supposedly to raise funds for a foreign war (even though the country was not fighting one at the time). His trial for non-payment was one of the events leading to the English Civil War.

Turn left along the minor road to reach the A4010 by the Bernard Arms – a pub with a wide selection of beers and food. Inside there is a collection of books, and there are various enlarged photographs on the walls.

Turn right along the A4010 to get back to the start.

WALK 12 – COOMBE AND WHITELEAF HILLS

DISTANCE :	**12km/7½ miles**
TIME:	**3 hours 30 mins**
MAP:	**OS Landranger 165, OS Explorer 181**
START :	**National Trust car park at Coombe Hill (Grid Ref 852063)**
REFRESHMENTS:	**The Plough, Lower Casden**

Head into the Chilterns with a walk starting from the popular Coombe Hill. Along the chalk escarpment and through beech-woods, this walk shows in a nutshell what the Chilterns have to offer.

START: The National Trust car park at Coombe Hill (grid ref 852063). It is situated at a right-angled bend in the lane to Dunsmore. From Wendover, the start is reached by proceeding west along the Ellesborough road (past the station). At Butlers Cross, turn left (signposted to Great Missenden), and after a short climb turn left along the lane signposted to Dunsmore, climbing up to the ridge-top.

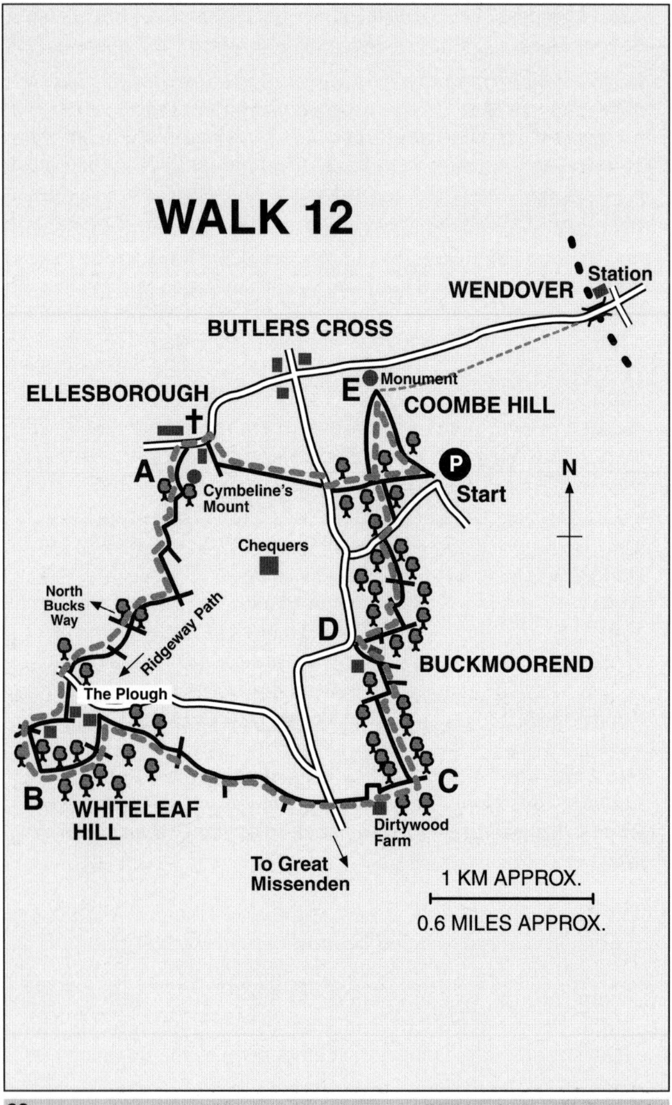

WALK 12

Station
WENDOVER

BUTLERS CROSS

ELLESBOROUGH

E ● Monument
COOMBE HILL

A

Cymbeline's
Mount

P
Start

N

Chequers

North
Bucks
Way

Ridgeway Path

D

The Plough

BUCKMOOREND

B
WHITELEAF
HILL

C

Dirtywood
Farm

To Great
Missenden

1 KM APPROX.

0.6 MILES APPROX.

Buses stop at Ellesborough. The walk can also be started from Wendover station (Chiltern Railways) by following the Ridgeway Path up to the monument at Coombe Hill.

THE WALK: From the car park bear left along by a fence on your left. The Coombe Hill monument is visited at the end of the walk. After the Ridgeway Path goes off to the right continue straight on downhill. This is a steep descent, and a trekking pole might come in useful in less than dry conditions. Near to the bottom, continue straight on over a track, down to a road.

Turn right along this road, then turn left at a public footpath sign. Cross this large field to the hedge corner, climbing gently. The path is usually well defined. Turn right at a T-junction to reach the village of Ellesborough.

Ellesborough is a tiny village with some thatched cottages and a church on a mound standing sentinel across the Vale of Aylesbury. The village is in the shadow of the Chiltern escarpment. Behind is Cymbeline's Mount – an Iron Age hill fort.

The church was built in both Decorated and Perpendicular styles, although it was restored during Victorian times. Inside, the nave was built using white Totternhoe stone. The church is not usually open.

(A) Turn left along the road (past the bus stop) and turn left through a kissing gate. Cross the field to a stile, then bear right, round the base of Cymbeline's Mount. The route of the path is faintly traced in the grass. Later follow a terrace path round the scarp to a stile. Follow the path through the trees.

After climbing some steps, cross the field to the trees ahead, where the path bends right. After crossing a drive, turn right along a small path (by the fence on your right). Turn left over the next stile (with the fence now on your left) to reach the Ridgeway Path.

The Ridgeway Path is the National Trail of the Chilterns. It runs for about 85 miles from Overton Hill, near Avebury, across the Wessex Downs, crossing Wiltshire and Berkshire (although the stretch past Whitehorse Hill and Waylands Smithy is now in Oxfordshire for administrative purposes) to Streatley, from where it follows the Chiltern escarpment to Ivinghoe Beacon.

Turn right at the cross-paths, following the Ridgeway along the escarpment. At a kissing gate, turn right down a sunken track. Turn left through a kissing gate, continuing to follow the Ridgeway. This point is the start of the North Bucks Way, which meanders its way across the Vale of Aylesbury. Follow the chalk track along the escarpment towards Whiteleaf Hill ahead. Continue straight on over a crossing footpath.

To the left is Pulpit Hill – now owned by the National Trust. It is a nature reserve, managed by BBONT (Buckinghamshire, Berkshire and Oxfordshire Naturalists' Trust). There is a hill fort on top, from which there are fine views across the Vale of Aylesbury (as there are from this part of the walk).

At a cross-paths, turn right along a bridleway for a few paces, then bear left onto a narrow path. Cross the field to a kissing gate leading into trees. Continue on down to the road at Lower Cadsden. Cross over the road and continue along by a fence on your left. At the fence corner, turn right across the golf course to a hedge gap. Pass along the left-hand edge of the cricket pitch (past the pavillion) to reach a lane. Turn left along this lane. Where the lane bends left towards the clubhouse, fork right into the woods. Cross over a track and, ignoring a path going off to the right (alongside a fence), go straight on up Whiteleaf Hill, heedless of all turnings off. After passing through a kissing gate, continue along the left-hand side of a meadow to the top.

From the top there is a superb view across Princes Risborough to the Bledlow Ridge. On the slope is Whiteleaf Cross, one of the earliest of the Chiltern hill marks. It was first documented in AD903 as a boundary mark. The cross may have been carved by monks later for devotional or navigational purposes.

(B) Turn left at the top, following the Ridgeway Path through Giles Wood. To the right is a tree-clad hollow known as The Hangings. Continue straight on over a cross-paths, straight on down the hill to The Plough.

The Plough is the only pub actually on the Ridgeway Path, and is popular with walkers. It is ideal for a lunch break (at about the halfway mark).

Claydon House, now a National Trust property (Walk 5)

River Chess near Latimer – only 30 miles from central London (Walk 15)

Picturesque cottages in the village of Little Missenden (Walk 17)

Hampden House, now a girls' school (Walk 18)

Turn right over a stile (by a public footpath/circular walk sign). Ignore a series of paths going off to the right when the path bears left. Later the path turns right and starts to climb. At a waymark post, turn left, climbing up to a clearing in the woods.

At the wood edge continue straight on over a track, and on along the right-hand edge of a field. The walk then carries straight on alongside a wood (on your right) and the right-hand edge of the next field to reach a track.

Turn left along this track. Cross over the road and continue along the drive to Dirtywood Farm opposite. Just before the farm buildings, turn left onto a permissive path round the edge of the garden (the official right of way passes close to the farmhouse).

Continue along the right-hand edge of the field, and follow a waymarked path up through the wood. **(C)** At the top of the rise turn sharp left along a waymarked path. Turn right at a T-junction at the wood edge. Ignore a path going off to the right, keeping to the path along the inside edge of the wood. Turn left along a lane, descending to the hamlet of Buckmoorend.

Buckmoorend consists of a farm and a few cottages built to house the workers on the Chequers Estate.

(D) At the end of the lane, turn right along a bridleway (now returning to thr Ridgeway Path). Where the track forks, take the right fork (following the Ridgeway waymark). Continue straight on over a track, leading up into the wood. At the top turn left onto a footpath, following a Ridgeway signpost. The walk now follows the Ridgeway back to the monument on Coombe Hill.

After about 20 yards, turn right by a signpost. Continue straight on over a bridleway. In the spring the ground becomes a sea of bluebells. Turn right over a stile in the fence, then turn left, proceeding in the same direction as before. Turn right along a lane. At the top turn left into the woods, following a path along the inside edge of the wood. At a kissing gate turn left (rejoining the outward route for a few paces), then turn right along the ridge to the monument – the climax of the walk.

As you walk along the ridge, there are superb views across to Ellesborough, Cymbeline's Mount and the Bledlow Ridge. Coombe Hill is the highest viewpoint of the Chilterns. Contrary to popular belief, it is not the highest point of the Chilterns, the actual Chiltern summit is in Wendover Woods, on the other side of the Misbourne Gap.

The monument was erected in memory of the men of Buckinghamshire killed in the Boer War. From here, there are wide wiews across the Vale of Aylesbury. In the front of the monument is a topograph. During the winter, sheep graze on the downland turf.

(E) From the monument, head south along the ridge-top (scrub on your right). Later the path bears left through some trees. Continue across the downland back to the start.

WALK 13 – WENDOVER WOODS

DISTANCE:	**14km/9 miles**
TIME:	**3 hours 30 mins**
MAP:	**OS Landranger 165, OS Explorer 181**
START:	**Car park at Aston Hill (Grid Ref 892102)**
REFRESHMENTS:	**Old Swan, Kingswood (short detour)**

An introduction to Wendover Woods, one of the largest Forestry Commission woodlands in the Chilterns. There is a selection of forest walks, horse trails, mountain biking trails and a fitness trail laid out in the woods.

START: Car park at Aston Hill (grid ref 892102). The car park is reached from Tring by proceeding westwards along the A41 towards Aylesbury, then turning left along the A4010. Turn left again on a minor road signposted to Cholesbury, climbing Aston Hill. The car park is on the left near the top. For public transport users, the walk can be accessed from Wendover station (the Chiltern line from Marylebone) via the Ridgeway Trail.

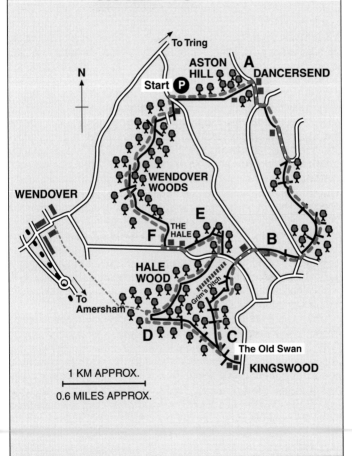

WALK 13

To Tring

ASTON HILL

A

DANCERSEND

Start **P**

N

WENDOVER WOODS

E

F

THE HALE

B

HALE WOOD

Grim's Ditch

To Amersham

D

C

The Old Swan

KINGSWOOD

WENDOVER

1 KM APPROX.

0.6 MILES APPROX.

From the car park at Aston Hill, there is a superb view across the Vale of Aylesbury, with the Wilstone and Marsworth reservoirs in the foreground. Aston Hill was part of Lord Rothschild's estate, and from 1904–25 was a famous motoring venue. Lionel Martin made his first ascent up Aston Hill in a tuned Singer car on 4 April 1914. He was so succesful at hill-climbing that a sporting light car was registered in his name in March 1915 called – Aston Martin. The rest is motoring history.

THE WALK: From the car park, proceed eastwards along a track. Ignore various footpaths going off into the woods. At Aston Hill Farm bear left into the woods and follow the footpath downhill. At the bottom turn right along Dancer's End Lane.

(A) Turn left at a T-junction (by the parish notice board). Where the lane bends left, turn right down a path between trees. Continue straight on over a cross-paths. Later the path becomes a lane. To the left is a fine view across to Ivinghoe Beacon.

When the lane bends left, turn right into the woods along a bridleway. Fork left onto a smaller path, past a Pavis Wood sign, climbing up the escarpment. Ignore a path going off to the left. At the top, go straight on over the Ridgeway Path. On leaving the wood, continue straight on across the field (the path is well defined at the time of writing). After a while the path swings left to a stile. After crossing a lane, continue straight on along the left-hand side of the field opposite (following a waymark arrow).

The path continues into Buckland Wood. At a cross-paths (with a waymark post) bear right. Fork right at the top of a rise, a waymark arrow confirming the route. Ignore a path going off to a stile on the left. At a cross-tracks continue straight on to reach a road.

(B) Cross over the road and bear right across the field opposite (by a stile/public footpath sign), rising gently to a hedge gap by a tree. Continue straight on across the next field to a stile to the right of a mobile home park. Where the fence bends left, continue straight on across the field to a stile ahead. Bear left through the mobile home park to reach a road.

Go straight on along Taylor's Lane opposite (signposted to The Hale). At a T-junction continue along a forest track opposite, rising gently across some heathland.

To the right of the walk (although not visible from the path) is part of Grim's Ditch – a Saxon earthwork across the Chilterns (see Introduction). The stretch to the northwest of the walk at this point is one of the best preserved sections.

After a crossing track, take the left fork. At a T-junction turn right along a forest ride. Ignore a path going off to the right when the path swings left. Later the path bears left to a T-junction. Turn left here, over a crossing track and on across the next field. Bear left across the next field to a hedge gap near the wood corner. Follow a waymarked path through the wood. At the wood edge, turn left along a track to reach the Old Swan pub at Kingswood, ideal for a break, at about the halfway mark.

(C) To resume the walk, retrace your steps along the track, then bear right back into the wood, following a public footpath sign. Continue straight on over a cross-tracks. Keep to the main path when a similar path goes off to the right at a field corner. Ignore a path going off into the woods just before an OS trig point.

A trig point in the middle of the woods? It is at the top of a gentle rise, so it must have offered a viewpoint across the group of villages and hamlets collectively called The Lee before the trees of Great Widmer Wood were planted.

Continue straight on over a second cross-paths. Soon after a small path merges from the right, turn right down a narrow path by a waymark arrow on a tree. **(D)** Turn right along the Ridgeway Path (where public transport users pick up the walk. For Wendover, turn left along the Ridgeway Path and follow the acorn waymarks back to the town and station.) The walk follows the Ridgeway Path for the next 1½ miles, heedless of all turnings off.

At a road, turn right, then left, still following the Ridgeway. Continue straight on over a cross-paths. Soon after, a fine vista across the Misbourne Valley opens out to the left. Soon, the Ridgeway Path turns left, descending. **(E)** At the bottom, turn left along a path (between a fence and a sunken track). The walk leaves the Ridgeway Path at this point.

After a while the path merges with the track. Follow this track down to a group of houses called The Hale. Turn right along the lane at the bottom.

(F) At a public footpath sign turn right along a forest track. Bear left onto a narrow path along by a fence on your left. Turn left up a track, heedless of all turnings off, climbing up through Wendover Woods. Near the top turn right at a T-junction.

At the top, cross over a track to a 'Fitness Trail' notice, and continue along the terrace path. Where the track forks, take the right fork, following a green waymark.

Later, a picnic site is reached in a clearing with fine views across Wendover to Coombe Hill. A recently built topograph points out the landmarks visible.

Follow this terrace path northwards along the edge of Haddington Hill, ignoring all paths leading off up and down the slope. Turn left at a T-junction.

By a waymark post turn right up some steps. Continue straight on over a road (the road leading to the main Wendover Woods car park and various other small parking spots). When the path forks, take the right fork. Turn right along the track at the top. At Aston Hill Lodge, cross the road back to the start.

WALK 14 – CHESHAM RIDGES

DISTANCE:	**14km/9 miles**
TIME:	**4 hours**
MAP:	**OS Landranger 165, OS Explorer 181**
START :	**Chesham underground station (Grid Ref 961017)**
REFRESHMENTS:	**The Bell, Chartridge; The Blue Ball, Asheridge**

A real roller-coaster of a walk, west of Chesham across the ridges of Chartridge, Asheridge, Bellingdon and Hawridge by way of paths across farmland. There are a couple of good pubs around the halfway mark in Chartridge and Asheridge. The return is via the long and scenic Hawridge, while the final stretch offers a panoramic view across the town.

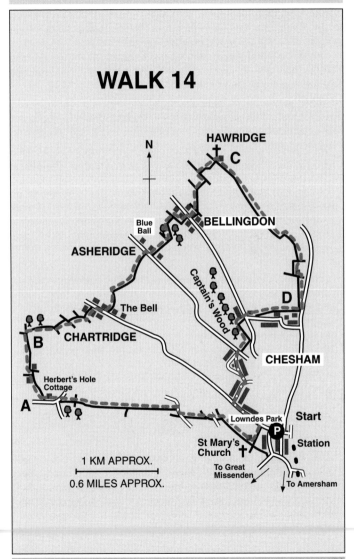

WALK 14

HAWRIDGE

N

C

Blue
Ball

BELLINGDON

ASHERIDGE

Captain's Wood

The Bell

D

B   CHARTRIDGE

CHESHAM

Herbert's Hole
Cottage

A

Lowndes Park   Start

St Mary's
Church   Station

To Great
Missenden

To Amersham

1 KM APPROX.

0.6 MILES APPROX.

START: Chesham underground station (grid ref 961017) – the terminus of the Metropolitan line, reached from Chalfont and Latimer station on a scenic single-track branch line. There are various car parks in the town itself (the Watermeadow car park at the southern end of the High Street – grid ref 958014 – is the largest and also the cheapest). Chesham is signposted from the A41 and A413, the main routes through the Chilterns to the north and south of the town.

THE WALK: From the station, turn left down a road leading to the town centre (opposite Boots). Turn right, then left by the war memorial leading to St. Mary's Way and Lowndes Park.

At first glance, Chesham appears to be a country market town with the Chilterns all around. However, it has a long connection with light industry, originally based in Waterside, at the southern end of the town, and more recently (in a case of bad town planning) there have been further developments towards Asheridge. There are some distinctive shops in the town centre, which is pedestrianised. The twice-weekly market has now moved into the High Street.

Chesham also has a large number of churches, covering a wide spectrum from Catholic to nonconformist. The main church, St. Mary's, is located on the southern edge of Lowndes Park, overlooking the town. The central tower has a slim lead spire, more in keeping with neighbouring Hertfordshire than Buckinghamshire. Inside on the east wall is a large wall-painting depicting the last days of Jesus by John Ward.

Cross over the road into Lowndes Park. Turn left along a metalled path above Scottowe's Pond. On the far side turn right along the Chiltern Link (passing St. Mary's church on your left) past the Guide Hut. Continue along the left-hand edge of the next field, bearing left to a stile.

The first part of the walk follows the Chiltern Link – a Buckinghamshire County Council recreational path linking the Chess Valley Walk, which follows the River Chess from Rickmansworth to Chesham, with the Ridgeway Path at Wendover.

After crossing the second stile, bear left (footpath to Pednor Road).

Cross the road and continue straight on (ignore a path going off to the right). Bear left in the second field to reach another lane. Turn right along this lane (ignore the path going straight on where the lane bends right), and turn left along Herbert's Hole – a track along the valley bottom. Continue straight on where the track bends left. Later there is a fence on the left, but the path continues along the valley bottom. **(A)** At the end of the track continue along a lane for a few paces, then turn right over a stile just after Herbert's Hole Cottage.

At the top turn left over a stile when the drive bends left. Almost immediately turn right over a stile, passing a pond on your right. Continue straight on after passing through a kissing gate. **(B)** Turn right over a stile into Bellows Wood and continue along the top edge of the wood. At the wood edge cross over a stile and follow the right-hand edge of the field round and down to a track, before climbing steeply up the other side. At the top continue straight on along a track, which later becomes a lane, to reach the modern settlement of Chartridge.

The villages of Chartridge, Asheridge, Bellingdon and Hawridge were originally built on the ridges because the valley bottoms were marshlands. The footpaths linking the ridges were once the only means of communication between the villages.

Turn right along the main road, then left by a public footpath sign (by the mission church). The Bell pub is a few yards further along the road. Continue along a narrow path between hedges, and later follow the right-hand edge of a field round to the left. At a hedge gap continue straight on across the field to a hedge corner ahead, and carry on along by a hedge (on your left) to reach a road in the village of Asheridge. The excellent Blue Ball pub is along the road to the left.

The main route, however, turns right along this road. Turn left along a farm drive by a public footpath sign (Widmore Farm). The path follows the right-hand edge of a field, then continues down through Widmore Wood. Where the path forks, take the left fork, crossing a track along the valley bottom to reach a stile at the wood edge. Continue up the left-hand edge of the field. At the top turn right along the top edge of the field. Pass through a kissing gate in the field corner and turn left to reach Bellingdon.

Turn right along the road through the village, then left along Ramscote Lane. Turn left over a stile just before Hilltop Farm, and bear right across the field to a hedge gap ahead, then straight on to another hedge gap ahead. Continue down the left-hand edge of the next field to a double stile in the valley bottom.

Turn left onto the path along the valley bottom. Just before the next stile turn right up the field (fence on your left) and go on along the right-hand edge of the next two fields.

Ahead is Hawridge, the prettiest of the villages on the Chesham Ridges. Hidden behind the trees is the small 13th-century church (St. Mary's again). Adjoining the church is Hawridge Court – built alongside a prehistoric earthwork. There are fine views as the walker returns towards Chesham along the ridge-top.

(C) At the top turn right over a stile. Continue along a grassy track between fields along the ridge-top. When the grassy track turns left in the second field, continue straight on to a hedge gap ahead. Follow the left-hand edge of the third field. Pass through a hedge gap in the field corner. After crossing over a stile, turn right to a second stile and continue down the left-hand edge of the next field to a track. Turn left along this track. Turn right over a stile along a path between fences leading back towards Chesham.

(D) Turn right along a track past Rickyard Barns. Continue straight on uphill, later between houses. At the top turn right, then left (past Nugent Court). Cross over a road (Mount Nugent) into Captain's Wood. Turn left along a path along the top edge of the wood. Turn right down some steps (by some wooden railings), with some houses on your left, descending steeply.

At the bottom continue straight on along Darvell Drive opposite (later Chapman's Crescent). To the left is a fine panoramic view across the town. At a T-junction turn right (along Penn Avenue). Turn left down Chartridge Lane back into the town centre. Retrace your steps back to the station.

WALK 15 – CHESS VALLEY

DISTANCE :	**11km/7 miles**
TIME:	**3 hours**
MAP:	**OS Landranger 165, OS Explorer sheets 172, 181 and 182**
START:	**Watermeadow car park at the southern end of Chesham (Grid Ref 958014)**
REFRESHMENTS:	**Swan and Crown pubs, overlooking Ley Common**

On the eastern fringes of Buckinghamshire, this walk explores the villages of Tyler's Hill and Ley Hill (Ley Hill is now a suburb of Chesham), before returning along the Chess Valley Walk – this is Metroland Chilterns. The Chess Valley Walk follows the River Chess between Rickmansworth and Chesham – linked to stations on the Metropolitan line (London underground).

START: The Watermeadow car park at the southern end of Chesham High Street (grid ref 958014). The walk can also be started from Chesham underground station (see Walk 14).

THE WALK: From the car park, turn right along the main road, passing the southern end of the High Street.

Chesham High Street has recently been pedestranised, the Market Square has been transformed and the clock tower has been rebuilt. There are some interesting shops in the High Street. Church Street, to the west of the High Street, contains an assortment of Georgian cottages. No 54/56 Church Street is believed to be the oldest cottage in Chesham. At the end of Church Street is the Queen's Head pub, which specializes in Thai cuisine.

Turn left along East Street. Bear right along Townfield and on up the steps crossing the railway. (From the station, turn left along the path alongside the railway, then left over the first bridge).

Turn right, then sharp left alongside an old railing to climb up out

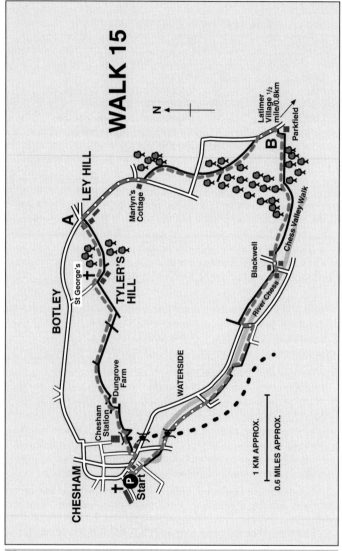

of the town. At the top continue straight on across the field, after pausing to admire a panoramic view across Chesham.

On the far side turn left (hedge on your right). Later cross over a stile and continue, with the hedge now on your left. On a clear day there is a wide view across the valley to the ridges on the west side of the town (explored in Walk 14).

Turn right at a T-junction, then at a gate turn left across the field to a stile. Continue straight on over a track, along by a hedge on your left. At a cross-paths continue straight on across the next field to a stile. The path is well defined, sometimes marked with intermittent groups of stones. Cross the next field to a stile in the field corner at the bottom.

Cross over a track and continue straight on up the other side (hedge on your left). Turn left at the top (towards Tyler's Hill). After crossing the next stile, continue across the field, passing to the left of a pub ahead (the Five Bells). **(A)** Turn right up the lane, passing St. George's church.

St. George's church was built in the 19th century (consecrated in 1871) as a satellite church of Christ Church in Waterside (the southern part of Chesham) to serve the villages of Botley and Ley Hill. Known as the 'Little Church in the Woods' because of its remote location, it now makes an ideal venue for a parish retreat.

At Cowcroft Farm turn left along a track through the woods, leading out to a quiet residential road in Ley Hill. At a T-junction turn right along the road past the Crown and Swan pubs.

Although Ley Hill is only about one-third of the way round the walk, the pubs here offer the last chance for refreshment before returning to Chesham. At least the walk is mainly level or down-hill from here, with only one gentle climb.

Turn left over a stile opposite Marlyn's Cottage. Follow the left-hand edge of the field. At the field corner turn left, then right over two stiles alongside a hedge on your right, climbing gently to a lane.

Turn left along this lane, then right over a stile into the woods. Follow a waymarked path through the wood (later to merge with a track). Turn left at a waymark post, and at a T-junction turn left to reach the wood edge. On leaving the wood bear right across the large field, passing to the left of an isolated barn, to reach a gate. Turn right along the lane towards the village of Latimer. **(B)** Where the lane bends left, turn right over a stile to join the Chess Valley Walk.

A ½ mile detour along the lane brings you to the pretty village of Latimer, with cottages around a triangular village green, down in the Chess Valley near the Hertfordshire Border. On the west side of the village, above the valley, is Latimer House, formerly owned by the Cavendish family – the Lords Chesham. Below the house, the River Chess has been dammed to make a tree-lined lake. The house is now owned by the Ministry of Defence. The church of St. Mary Magadelene nearby contains a memorial window to the Cavendish family. The church itself was rebuilt in the 19th century.

The path follows the left-hand edge of a large field. At the far corner, the path bears left through the wood (between fences) before descending to the valley. To the left is a fine view across the Chess Valley.

At the bottom continue along the left-hand edge of a series of fields to arrive at a lane. Here, turn left, then right by a public footpath/Chess Valley Walk sign to reach a stile. Continue along the left-hand edge of the next two fields to reach a stile leading to a road at a right-angled bend. Turn left along this road, then right along Holloway Lane.

Where the road bends left, continue straight on along a path sign-posted to Chesham Moor. Turn right through a kissing gate by a Chess Valley Waymark, following a path between fences. At the road, turn left along the riverside path. At a waterfall, turn left, then right imme-diately. Later, bear left to pass along the right-hand edge of a playing field (Chesham Moor). Continue straight on along Moor Road past a tennis court and swimming pool.

At a roundabout cross over the main road (there is a traffic island in the middle), and bear left by a public footpath sign into Meades Water Garden. Turn left over a footbridge by a brick-and-flint gazebo. Later the path turns right over a second footbridge, before turning left to reach Germain Street.

Back in the old part of Chesham, Germain Street contains some Georgian houses and a pub. The junction of Germain Street and Red Lion Street (the main road) has now been pedestrainised, making Germain Street much more peaceful.

Continue along Water Meadow back to the car park. For the station, turn right, then left along the High Street, past the Market Square. Turn right up a road (opposite Boots) to reach the station forecourt.

WALK 16 – CHALFONT AND SEER GREEN

DISTANCE:	**11km/7 miles**
TIME:	**3 hours**
MAP:	**OS Landranger 175, OS Explorer 172**
START:	**Car park in Chalfont St. Giles (Grid Ref 965910)**
REFRESHMENTS:	**Chalfont St. Giles**

On the edge of the Chilterns, this walk explores the Misbourne Valley and the model village of Jordans. There are wide views across the Misbourne Valley on the final descent from Hodgemoor Woods and after the initial climb through the outskirts of Chalfont St. Peter. The going tends to be more sticky after rain because there is now London clay underfoot rather than the Chiltern chalk.

START: The car park in the village of Chalfont St. Giles (grid ref 989935). The village is just off the main A413, southwest of a double roundabout at Pheasant's Hill (by the Citroen garage). The bus from Uxbridge to High Wycombe (305) stops in the village (approximately a two-hourly service). Alternatively, the walk can be reached from Seer Green station (grid ref 965910) on the Chiltern Railways line from Marylebone to High Wycombe.

THE WALK: Turn right out of the car park and go along the main street through the village past the village green.

Just yards from the main A413 road, Chalfont St. Giles has retained its village character. There are some red-brick and timber houses round the tiny village green. The village was home to the poet Milton and his family when they were evacuated during the

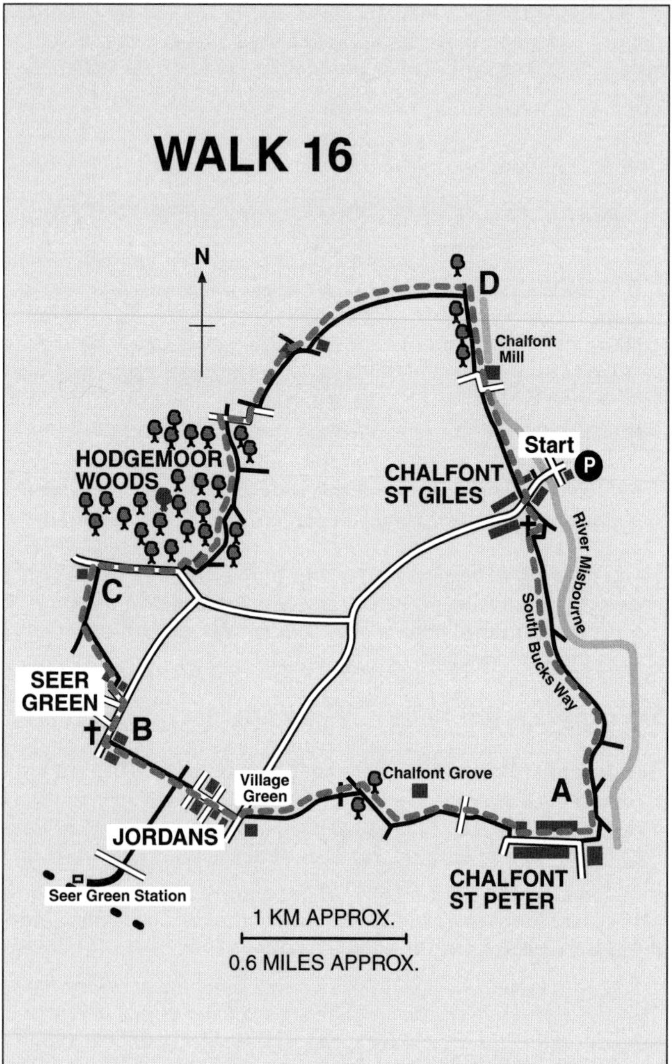

WALK 16

HODGEMOOR WOODS

CHALFONT ST GILES

Chalfont Mill

Start P

River Misbourne

South Bucks Way

C

SEER GREEN

B

Village Green

Chalfont Grove

A

JORDANS

Seer Green Station

CHALFONT ST PETER

1 KM APPROX.
0.6 MILES APPROX.

D

Plague in 1665. He finished 'Paradise Lost' and started 'Paradise Regained' here. The cottage where he stayed is now a museum.

St. Giles church is approached from the village street by a timber-framed lynchgate, incorporated in a house. The exterior was restored in 1663. Inside, the 13th-century chancel has a double piscina, and there is a 14th-century wall-painting depicting the life of Christ and the Virgin Mary. On the wall between the chancel and nave (the Chancel Arch) is the Lord's Prayer, the Ten Commandments and the Nicene Creed. The church is usually open 11am–4pm each day.

Turn left (opposite the Crown pub) through the lynchgate, passing to the right of the church (the South Bucks Way). Turn right over a stile (fence on your right), then turn right at a waymark post. At a T-junction turn left to follow the South Bucks Way along the Misbourne Valley.

The South Bucks Way is a Buckinghamshire County Council recreational route from the Ridgeway at Coombe Hill to the Grand Union Canal at Denham, a distance of 22 miles.

When open fields are reached, continue straight on along by a fence on your left. Later, ignore a path going off to the left, keeping to the South Bucks Way. Later, turn left over a stile, then turn right along by a fence on your right. When the path forks, bear right, passing to the right of some tennis courts to arrive at a recreation ground. Turn right along a path between fences and straight on up Boundary Road. **(A)** At the top turn right along a path between fences, passing to the left of a school. Looking back, there is a fine view across the Misbourne Valley. Cross over a road and continue along the path opposite (fence on your right). At a gate continue with a fence on your right to a stile, then turn right. Bear left across a lage field between trees.

Where the path bends right, continue straight on through a hedge gap to a stile, leading into the woods. On the far side of the wood turn left alongside a fence on your left. Cross over a drive, and go past a pylon on your left and fence on your right along the right-hand edge of the field opposite.

Bear right to a stile in the field corner, then continue along the right-hand edge of the next field by a wooden fence. Continue along a path between fences and a gravel drive to reach the village of Jordans. Cross over the road and carry straight on along Seer Green Lane opposite past Jordans village green (and an old-fashioned 'Give Way' sign).

Jordans is a 'purpose-built' village, designed by F. Rowantree in 1919, with Tudor-style cottages around the village green. Cricket has always been played on the village green, although more recently the villagers tried to get it stopped, because the improved design of modern cricket bats makes the ball travel further.

Some 400 yards to the south is the Quaker Meeting House, built in 1688. A nearby barn is said to contain timber from the 'Mayflower'. In the grounds of the meeting house are the plain graves of William Penn, Gulielma Penn, Isaac Pennington and Thomas Ellwood.

Continue straight on over the cross-roads on the far side of the green, descending to a track in the valley bottom (Seer Green station is ½ mile to the southwest along this track) and straight on up the other side. Turn left at a T-junction to reach the Seer Green.

(B) Turn right along the main road through the village, past the little flint church of Holy Trinity, built in 1847. Turn left along Howard Road, past a secondhand car showroom, then bear right along Howard Crescent.

Turn right along a path between fences (by No 18). At the end of the gardens bear left across a large field to a stile. Turn right along a path between fences, then along by a fence on your right and another fenced path to reach a lane. **(C)** Turn right along this lane. Where the lane bends right continue straight on over a stile, then turn right along the right-hand edge of a paddock.

Turn left over a stile (along by a fence on your left). Continue straight on past a large barn used as an indoor equestrian arena to enter Hodgemoor Woods. (Ignore a path going off to the right.)

Continue along a path, keeping to the inside edge of the wood. Where the path bends left, turn right to the wood edge and continue along the left-hand edge of two fields. Turn left, to re-enter the woods at a waymark post. Turn right at a T-junction along a main path. Follow the waymark arrows on trees, gently climbing up through the wood to reach a lane.

Turn right along this lane. Where the lane bends right continue straight on along the left-hand edge of a field.

At a track turn right, then left (signposted to London Road). Continue straight on down the right-hand edge of a series of fields. In the third field turn right over a stile, and bear right across the next field (continuing downhill) to a stile in the opposite fence. **(D)** After crossing a narrow tract of woodland turn right at a T-junction (back along the South Bucks Way).

By Chalfont Mill, continue along a lane. When the lane bends left carry straight on along a track leading back to Chalfont St. Giles centre. Turn left along the main road through the village back to the start.

WALK 17 – LITTLE MISSENDEN

DISTANCE :	**10km/6½ miles**
TIME:	**2 hours 30 mins**
MAP:	**OS Landranger 165, OS Explorer 172**
START:	**Lay-by at the entrance to Shardelodes (Grid Ref 947978)**
REFRESHMENTS:	**Red Lion and Crown pubs, Little Missenden**

Despite being sandwiched between two main roads, this is a peaceful stroll through some of the remotest countryside in Buckinghamshire.

START: The lay-by at the entrance to Shardeloes (grid ref 947978). It is reached from the roundabout at the western end of the Amersham by-pass (the A413). Buses stop in Amersham Old Town, from where the walk can be accessed by a footpath. Amersham station is at the end of the Metropolitan line, but it is in the new part of the town on the hill to the north.

THE WALK: From the lay-by head southwest along the drive to Shardeloes, climbing gently and passing the ground of Amersham

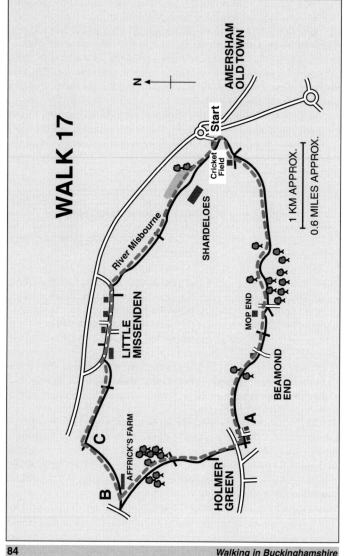

WALK 17

AMERSHAM
OLD TOWN

Start

Cricket
Field

SHARDELOES

River Misbourne

N

1 KM APPROX.

0.6 MILES APPROX.

LITTLE
MISSENDEN

MOP END

BEAMOND
END

AFFRICK'S FARM

HOLMER
GREEN

A

B

C

Cricket Club to the right. At the top of the rise, bear left through a kissing gate along the left-hand edge of a field, past a green arrow. Continue straight on, ignoring tracks going off right and left, keeping to the valley bottom.

Later turn right over a stile, following the path round the northern perimeter of an electricity sub-station. Fortunately, the sub-station is hidden from the path. At the top of the rise, the path leads out through woods to the hamlet of Mop End.

Cross over the lane and stile opposite and continue along by the hedge on your right (NOT the path across the middle of the field going off to the left). At a stile in the field corner, bear right across the field to a stile in the opposite fence. Cross over the track and continue along the left-hand side of the field opposite leading to a farm at Beamond End.

Turn left along a lane, then turn right over a stile and continue along the right-hand edge of the next field. At a hedge corner continue straight on downhill to a stile. Follow the path through the wood and on between fences, dropping down to the valley bottom and on up the other side to reach Holmer Green.

(A) Turn right at a T-junction, then left by a public footpath sign. Turn right at a cross-paths (by a 'No Cycling' sign). Continue past some garages to reach a road.

Cross over a road and continue along the grassy track between hedges opposite. After crossing over a stile continue along by a hedge on the right. At the hedge corner bear left across the field to a stile in the opposite corner. Carry on along the left-hand side of the next field. At the field corner cross over a track and continue down the path opposite (alongside a track). Later cross over a stile and turn right down this track, which descends to a valley bottom before climbing up to Affrick's Farm.

(B) At the top turn sharp right along a metalled drive. Pass to the left of some farm buildings. Pass through a kissing gate and continue along the right-hand edge of a paddock. At a kissing gate in the corner of the second field turn right, then left along the left-hand edge of the next field. Ahead is a fine vista along the Misbourne Valley back towards Amersham.

At a hedge corner continue straight on, bearing slightly right up to the ridge-top (to join the South Bucks Way). **(C)** Turn right along

The church at Little Missenden: the village itself has been spared development and retains its peaceful character

the South Bucks Way along the ridge-top, and continue along the left-hand edge of the next field. At a crossing track continue straight on across the next field, following the telegraph lines to reach the village of Little Missenden. (The South Bucks Way turns right along the crossing track to by-pass the village.) Turn right along the road through the village.

Little Missenden is a pretty village, which has been by-passed by both the A413 and the railway, thus retaining its peaceful village character, and has been saved developments such as those in neighbouring Amersham and Great Missenden.

The church of St. John the Baptist has an Anglo-Saxon nave, with a chancel added in the 13th century and a north chapel in the 14th century. A south porch was added in the 15th century, and this was the last addition to the church until the vestry was added in 1980. Inside there are some wall-paintings which were uncov-

ered in 1931. Although only parts of the paintings have been preserved they are interesting. They include St. Christopher carrying the Christ-child, scenes from the martyrdom of St. Catherine, the passion of Christ, parts of the Nativity, Christ in majesty and the Crucifixion. The gates were one of the earliest memorials to Dunkirk erected at an English church.

Further along the village road are two fine pubs, the Red Lion and the Crown. Both pubs offer a good range of beers and food – ideal for a stop before the final stretch along the Misbourne Valley back to Amersham.

Just after the Crown, where the road bends left, continue straight on by a public footpath/South Bucks Way sign. Where the track bends left continue straight on through a gate. At a cross-tracks continue straight on (footpath to Amersham). The path is well defined. Later bear left to a stile and carry straight on along the left-hand edge of the next field. Up on the hill to the right is Shardeloes.

Shardeloes was built in the 18th century for William Drake, the then MP for Amersham. It is one and a half stories high with a top balustrade. On the north side (visible from the walk) is a great portico with some Corinithian columns. Below the house is a large ornamental lake. Today the house has been converted into luxury apartments.

At the end of the field cross over a stile and continue along a path between fences. Bear left, passing to the left of a club house. Follow a track round the left-hand edge of the cricket field, back to the Shardeloes drive. Turn left here, back to the start.

WALK 18 – THE HAMPDEN COUNTRY

DISTANCE :	**13.5km/8½ miles (longer walk); 10km/6 miles (shorter route via Great Hampden)**
TIME:	**3 hours 30 mins (longer walk); 2 hours 30 mins (shorter walk)**
MAP:	**OS Landranger 165, OS Explorer 181**
START :	**Opposite the Rising Sun pub at Little Hampden (Grid Ref 856040)**
REFRESHMENTS:	**Rising Sun, Little Hampden; Hampden Arms, Great Hampden; Pink and Lily, Parslows Hillock (longer walk)**

This walk goes through the Hampden Country – one of the best walking areas in the Chilterns, a combination of pastoral farm-land, rolling hills and beechwoods.

START: The walk starts at Little Hampden (grid ref 856040). It is one of the remotest hamlets in Buckinghamshire, being situated at the end of a long and winding narrow lane. At the start is the Rising Sun – a pub whose remote location makes it the Chilterns equivalent of an Alpine mountain restaurant.

Little Hampden is reached from Great Missenden by heading northwest from the roundabout in the village centre (not the A4128 towards Wycombe), then turning left along Rignall Road over the railway (and past Wicks' Motors) along the Hampden Valley. Little Hampden is along the second lane after Little Honor End Farm (the Rising Sun is signposted).

The High Wycombe to Speen bus stops at Great Hampden at 9.50am (the last morning bus leaves High Wycombe at 9.30am). A bus leaves Great Hampden at 1.50pm, and Monday–Friday there is a later bus in the afternoon. There is no Sunday service.

THE WALK: From the Rising Sun turn sharp right down the path by a public footpath sign (NOT the bridleway). Follow the path through the wood. Later merge with a track (hedge on the left). In the valley

WALK 18

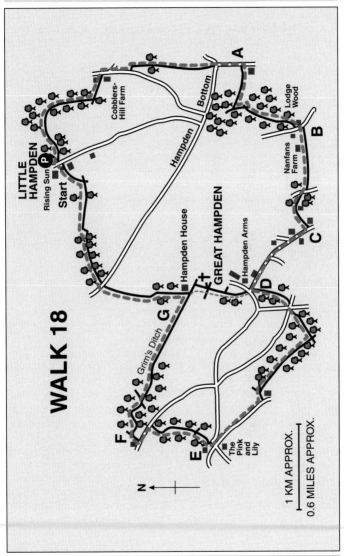

LITTLE HAMPDEN

Rising Sun

P

Start

Cobblers-Hill Farm

Hampden Bottom

Lodge Wood

B

Nanfans Farm

A

GREAT HAMPDEN

Hampden House

Hampden Arms

C

D

Grim's Ditch

G

F

E

The Pink and Lily

N

1 KM APPROX.

0.6 MILES APPROX.

bottom turn left into the woods, then turn right immediately along the inside edge of the wood. At the wood corner continue straight on up the ridge, passing a pit on your left. Turn right along the ridge-top.

Looking back there is a fine view across the valley to Little Hampden, with the Rising Sun in among the trees. There are further views across the Hampden Country as you proceed along the ridge-top through Hampdenleaf Wood.

Turn left at a cross-paths (by a waymark post). After leaving the wood bear right across the field in the direction of a waymark arrow to two stiles opposite. Continue along a drive. Turn right down a lane at a cross-roads, ignoring a lane going off to the left. Where the lane bends right turn left by a public footpath sign along a track between hedges, then along the right-hand edge of the field. The path continues through the wood and on down the right-hand edge of the next field. Bear left across a large field, heading downhill to the road junction in the valley. Go straight on up the road opposite. **(A)** Turn right up some steps by a public footpath sign and on along the right-hand edge of the field (further views to the right).

The path continues through the wood. Ignore a cross-tracks. At a T-junction turn left, starting to climb. At a cross-paths in a small clearing turn right (waymark arrow on tree). Continue straight on over the next two cross-paths. Bear right (by a waymark arrow on a tree) to reach a road. Turn left along this road. Turn right along the drive to Nanfans Farm (by a public footpath sign).

(B) Where the drive bends right, continue staight on over a stile. At the next stile go straight on across the field to a further stile and on through some scrub. Later there is a fence on your left. In the next field continue straight on to the left-hand end of the spinney ahead, then bear right down the field to some steps by a public footpath sign. Turn right along the road for a few paces, then turn left into the woods by a public footpath sign. Continue straight on over a drive. At the top, merge with this drive. Bear right to a path between a fence and hedge, passing round the Old Rectory. Continue straight on along a track. **(C)** Turn right along a lane towards Great Hampden (past a pretty cottage on your left). Bear left where the lane forks. At a road corner continue straight on along the road, past the cricket pitch to Great Hampden and the excellent Hampden Arms pub.

(D) For a **shorter walk**, continue straight on over the T-junction (by the Hampden Arms) along a track. Turn right by a public footpath sign through a kissing gate. The path follows the wood edge, then crosses the fields to reach Great Hampden church. Ignore all turnings off. Pass to the left of the church, then turn left along the drive to Great Hampden House. Pass through a gate, then immediately turn right over a stile to rejoin the main route.

(D) For the main route turn left by the bus stop along the right-hand edge of the cricket field, and follow the path down through the wood (near the right-hand edge) to a gate. Turn right along a road at the bottom. At a cross-roads bear left into the wood by a public bridleway sign. Follow the footpath (fence on the left – the walkers and riders are kept apart) up through the wood. At the top of the rise continue straight on over a cross-paths.

Turn right at a cross-paths at the wood edge. At the wood corner turn left along a track to leave the wood. Turn right along a lane, rising gently to Parslow's Hillock and the Pink and Lily pub.

The Pink and Lily is an excellent pub, offering a wide range of beers and food. It was originally named after a Mr Pink and a Miss Lily, a butler and parlourmaid at the nearby Hampden House (maybe they set up as publicans after leaving service). A regular drinker there was the poet Rupert Brooke. When the pub became a free house in the 1980s it was refurbished and a conservatory added.

(E) Where the road bends right, turn left along a track leading to Hampden Lodge. Turn right into the woods by a public bridleway sign. Continue straight on over a cross-paths following a blue waymark arrow. Later the path swings right and continues between fences to reach a road. Turn left along this road, **(F)** then right by a public footpath sign along a track between a cottage and a post box. At the end of the track bear right into the woods following a waymark arrow. Cross over a track, then at a T-junction turn left along a forest track (the footpath is signposted).

Soon after a track merges from the right, turn right up a small path (past a waymark arrow on a tree). Continue straight on over a track at the top of the rise. Continue straight on at the next cross-tracks. At the wood corner turn left, then right along a waymarked path through a strip of woodland.

This section of the walk follows part of the Saxon earthwork Grim's Ditch.

Continue straight on along a track between fields. Where the track bends right, continue straight on through a gate. **(G)** Just before Hampden House turn left over a stile. The short walk rejoins the main walk at this point.

Great Hampden church and House have been owned by the Hampden family since the 11th century. The most (in)famous of the Hampden clan was John Hampden, cousin of Oliver Cromwell, whose refusal to pay Ship Money – a tax imposed by Charles I – was one of the events leading to the Civil War. He even rallied support for his cause by riding his horse down to Great Kimble church one Sunday, disrupting the morning service. Despite this, he was buried in St. Mary Magdalen church opposite the house. The house itself was rebuilt in a Gothic style in the 18th century and is now a girls' school. The house and grounds are separated from the adjoining field by a ha-ha – a deep ditch which, from a distance, gives the impression that the gardens and field are continuous.

Cross the field, passing Hampden House on the right, to a stile in the opposite fence. Continue downhill through the wood (between fences). At the bottom continue straight on across a large field to the opposite corner, following a series of white posts.

Cross over the road and continue along a path through the strip of wood opposite. After the path bends left turn right through a hedge gap (by a yellow arrow). Bear right across the field, climbing to a gap in the opposite hedge. Continue climbing through the trees. At the top bear slightly right across a large field. Turn left at a cross-paths in the middle of the field to a hedge gap. Continue along a path between a hedge and fence, then along a drive back to the hamlet of Little Hampden. Turn left along the lane back to the start.

WALK 19 – HUGHENDEN

DISTANCE:	12½km/8 miles
TIME:	3 hours
MAP:	OS Landranger 165, OS Explorer 172
START:	Car park by Hughenden church (Grid Ref 864955)
REFRESHMENTS:	The Harrow, Upper Hughenden Valley; tea rooms at Hughenden Manor

Based around the National Trust property of Hughenden Manor, this walk explores the rolling farmland and wooded ridges north of High Wycombe. The ever-changing scenery makes for several views to enjoy.

START: The car park by Hughenden church (grid ref 864955). It is reached from High Wycombe by proceeding northwards on the A4128 towards Prestwood for about 1½ miles. Hughenden Manor is signposted from the road. Buses from High Wycombe stop outside.

THE WALK: From the car park head west through the churchyard, passing to the left of the church. Continue across the field to a gate (with a cattle grid) and on up the drive to Hughenden Manor.

Hughenden church was rebuilt in the 19th century, with only the 14th-century north chapel remaining from the original church. Inside is a memorial to Benjamin Disraeli, prime minister and statesman, who lived at the manor and is buried in the churchyard against the east end. This is the only memorial erected to a subject by a reigning monarch. In the chancel are some Victorian wall-paintings which have recently been restored. The stained-glass windows largely feature angels (the full name of the church is St. Michael and all Angels).

Disraeli bought Hughenden in 1848 and rebuilt the manor in its present 'Jacobean' form. The manor has been owned by the National Trust since 1946. The house now contains much Disraeli memorabilia, together with a number of paintings of Disraeli and

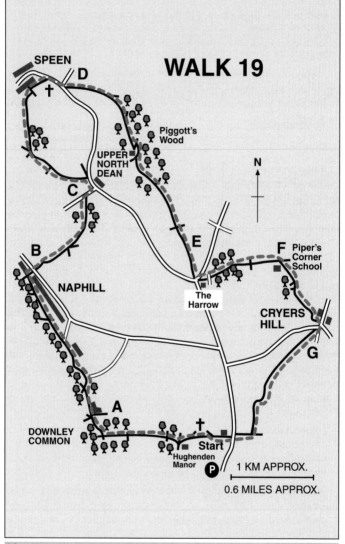

WALK 19

SPEEN

D

†

Piggott's
Wood

UPPER
NORTH
DEAN

C

N

B

NAPHILL

E

F Piper's
Corner
School

The
Harrow

CRYERS
HILL

G

A

DOWNLEY
COMMON

†

Start

Hughenden
Manor

P

1 KM APPROX.

0.6 MILES APPROX.

his family, the royal family and his political collegues. He often held political meetings at Hughenden. The house is open from April to October daily, except Monday and Tuesday 1–5pm (although details may vary from year to year). Details on 01494 755565.

Where the drive bends left, continue straight on down a bridleway signposted to Downley. Ignore a crossing path and continue between fences to reach another wood. Ignore a path going off to the left. **(A)** Turn right at a cross-tracks (by a National Trust sign) to climb up to Downley Common. Cross the common to reach a track alongside the houses ahead. Carry along this track, passing to the left of these houses. Continue straight on through the woods, passing a pit on your left.

When a further lane is reached, continue along it, passing to the left of the houses. Bear right to a brick-and-flint cottage and continue along a more solid track. Continue straight on along the edge of the common when this track bends right. Ignore a footpath with a 'No Cycling' sign and various paths going off into the woods on the left. **(B)** Later turn right along a path between hedges marked with a waymark arrow and another 'No Cycling' sign. Next to this path is a pair of semi-detached cottages.

Cross over the road and continue straight on over the stile opposite to a stile by a gate. Cross the next field. On the far side of this field turn left for a few paces, then bear right across the next field to a stile in the opposite corner. Follow the path through the wood. Later the path bends left and starts to descend. Bear right to a smaller path (twin waymark arrows on trees). On leaving the wood cross the field to a stile in the opposite fence. Turn right down the lane. At a T-junction at the bottom turn left along the road through the hamlet of Upper North Dean.

Upper North Dean, like its hilltop neighbour Speen, consists of various attractive houses with an enviable location – Speen, in particular, has wide views all around. From Upper North Dean there is a fine view down the Hughenden Valley.

(C) Bear left along a track by a telephone box (just before a single-track road sign). After crossing a stile turn left to a further stile and cross the field. Continue along the valley (later pass to the left of a

Hughenden Manor, the former home of Benjamin Disraeli

line of trees). In the next field follow a hedge (on your left) to reach a stile in the wood corner. Turn right, climbing up the inside edge of the wood. Continue along the left-hand edge of the field to reach the top of the hill. To the left are the houses of Speen.

At the top turn left along a track, then right alongside some gardens. Later continue between fences to reach a drive. Turn left to reach the road through the village.

Turn right along this lane, passing the Baptist church. **(D)** When Spring Coppice Lane is reached, bear left over a stile. Climb up across two fields to reach a track between hedges leading to Piggott's Wood. When this track bends left continue straight on over a stile along the top edge of two fields. From here there is a fine view across Lower North Dean.

On entering Piggott's Wood continue straight on along the ridge-top through the wood, ignoring all turnings off. When a shed is reached turn left, then sharp right along a drive. Turn left along a path by a public footpath sign (just after a stained-glass studio). Where the track bends left continue straight on along a smaller path (faint

St. Bartholomew's church, Fingest (Walks 22 and 23)

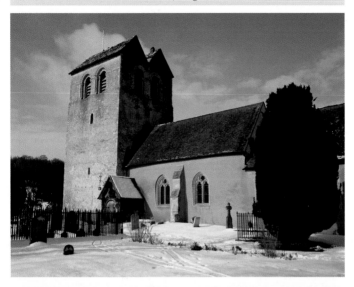

Autumn colours of Great Wood near Hambleden (Walk 24)

Brick and flint cottages in Hambleden (Walks 24 and 25)

Hambleden church, the cathedral of the Chilterns (Walks 24 and 25)

waymark arrow on tree) to reach a stile at the wood edge. Ahead is one of the finest views in the district, as you look along the length of the Hughenden Valley.

Continue straight on down the field, bearing right to a stile at the bottom. Carry straight on over a crossing track across the field to reach the Harrow pub.

(E) Turn left across the pub car park and go on along a path between fences. Cross over a road and continue straight on up a path between fences. This is a steep climb, but there are some steps built into the hillside to assist you. At the top the effort is rewarded with a fine view across to Piggott's Wood.

Ignore a crossing path at the top of the hill. At a stile continue straight on across the next field, then along by a fence on your right. **(F)** Turn right over a stile in the fence, then across a drive (leading to Piper's Corner, an independent girls' school). Cross over a further drive and on along the left-hand edge of the field opposite. Ignore two paths going off to the right in Gomm's Wood. Continue along the left-hand edge of a field, then between fences to reach the A4128 at Cryers Hill. On the left is a general stores.

(G) Turn right along this road, then at a public footpath sign bear left along the top edge of the fields. Continue along a path between fences, first through some scrub, then between fields. At the end of this path you are greeted with a fine view across to Hughenden Church, the Manor hidden in the trees on the ridge opposite.

Turn right along the right-hand edge of a large field. At a T-junction turn right down to the road. Turn left along this road, then right along the drive to Hughenden Manor back to the start.

WALK 20 – WEST WYCOMBE AND BRADENHAM

DISTANCE:	**14km/9 miles**
TIME:	**3 hours 30 mins**
MAP:	**OS Landranger 165, OS Explorer 172**
START :	**Public car park next to West Wycombe garden centre (Grid Ref 826947)**
REFRESHMENTS:	**Red Lion, Bradenham; West Wycombe**

West Wycombe is an attractive village, now owned by the National Trust. This easy-to-follow walk follows the ridge along to Saunderton, before returning along the other side of the A4010 via Bradenham, Disraeli's birthplace.

START: The large public car park next to the garden centre in West Wycombe (grid ref 826947). It is reached from High Wycombe by taking the A40 westwards towards Stokenchurch. West Wycombe is at the end of the built-up area. Regular buses from High Wycombe stop at West Wycombe.

THE WALK: From the car park cross over the road and proceed along a well-worn path. When the path forks, continue straight on, climbing up towards the ridge. There are steps built into the hillside to assist you on the steepest part. Turn left towards the mausoleum.

Behind the mausoleum is the Georgian church with its famous 'Golden Ball' – one of the many Chiltern landmarks. The mausoleum, like the Golden Ball, is set on the axis of the road to High Wycombe, built by Sir Francis Dashwood with chalk excavated from the nearby caves (passed on the final stretch of the walk). These caves were the venue for Dashwood's exclusive Hell Fire Club, formed after the Monks of Medmenham was disbanded. The Hell Fire Club (whose motto was 'Do what you will') contained some influential men of the time, including John

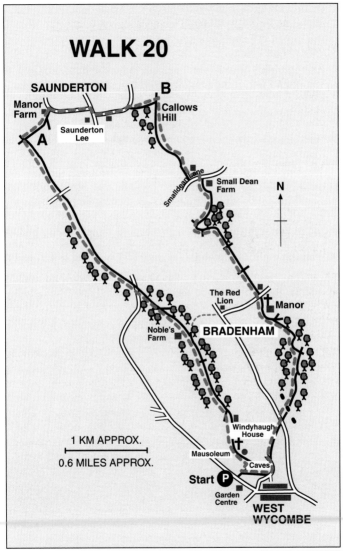

WALK 20

SAUNDERTON

Manor
Farm

A

Saunderton
Lee

B

Callows
Hill

Smalldean Lane

Small Dean
Farm

N

The Red
Lion

Manor

Noble's
Farm

BRADENHAM

Windyhaugh
House

Mausoleum

Caves

1 KM APPROX.

0.6 MILES APPROX.

Start **P**

Garden
Centre

WEST
WYCOMBE

Wilkes (MP for Aylesbury) and Lord Sandwich (then chancellor of the exchequer). Though much debauchery went on at meetings of the Hell Fire Club, rumours of devil-worship were somewhat exaggerated.

West Wycombe church was originally medieval, but was largely rebuilt and refurnished by Dashwood in Georgian times. The fittings were influenced by the pagan tendencies of the Hell Fire Club. The Golden Ball was fitted with a table and chairs, and was used for meetings of the inner circle of the club. The mausoleum was built in 1752 to house the bodies of Hell Fire Club members.

Pass to the right of the church and mausoleum through the churchyard. On the far side of the churchyard turn right to reach the National Trust car park. Cross the car park, making for a track passing to the left of Windyhaugh House ahead. Follow this path along the length of the ridge, heedless of all turnings off. As you proceed along the ridge there are fine views across to the Bledlow Ridge, left and Bradenham, right. Hearnton Wood is a mix of beech trees and pines.

Dashwood Mausoleum, where members of the Hell Fire Club were laid to rest

Later a rebuilt farmhouse (Noble's Farm) is reached, and the track becomes metalled. To the right is a footpath descending down the ridge, leading directly to Bradenham. Follow this metalled drive through the woods and down to the road at Slough Bottom. Cross over the road and continue along the left-hand edge of the field opposite to the summit of Slough Hill. Descend via the left-hand edge of a second field to reach another road. To the right is a fine view across to Lacey Green and Whiteleaf Hill, even though the vista is somewhat marred by the factory in the valley.

Cross the road and continue along the right-hand edge of the field opposite. Ahead is Lodge Hill and to the left, a closer view of the Bledlow Ridge. **(A)** In the second field turn right over a stile after passing underneath a pylon line (fence now on your left). Cross over a stile by a pylon and continue (hedge now on your right). By a gate bear left across the field to a stile to the left of some trees and to the right of a house, leading out to the road.

Turn right along this road, then right along the slip road to reach the A4010. Cross over the A4010 and turn left along a lane signposted to Loosley Row. When the road bends left, turn right to a couple of stiles, and continue straight on up the hill. **(B)** At the top turn right over a stile through some trees. To the right is a superb view across the valley to Lodge Hill and the Bledlow Ridge.

On leaving the woods continue along the left-hand edge of three fields, descending to a lane in Smalldean Bottom. Turn left along this lane then right through Small Dean Farm, following a public footpath sign. The path follows the edge of Park Wood. A steepish climb is rewarded with another fine view across the valley. Soon Bradenham comes into view. At a cross-paths the path leaves Park Wood and continues across the fields to Bradenham.

Bradenham (also owned by the National Trust) is dominated by a flint church and a red-brick manor house at the top of a large village green. The village houses are along the road leading to the Red Lion pub at the junction with the A4010.

The manor house (which is not open to the public) was owned by Isaac d'Israeli (father of Benjamin Disraeli). The manor was originally Tudor, but was rebuilt in its present classical style in 1620. The church was restored by G.E. Street in 1863. The east window of the chapel contains a crest of Lord Thomas of

Windsor, an early owner of the manor. This is an early example of stained glass. The chancel screen is a 20th-century addition. Inside is a series of paintings depicting the Crucifixion. The lynch-gate was built in 1920 to commemorate the men of the village who died in the 1914–18 war.

Cross the village green in front of the church and the ornamental gate and iron railings of the manor house. On the far side of the green turn left along a track, passing the grounds of the manor on your left. At a left-hand bend, fork right into the woods. Follow the waymarked path through the wood. The path merges with a track before descending to a dip and climbing up the other side. At a T-junction at the top of the wood turn right. When the track bends left, continue straight on along a narrower (waymarked) path. The path then bears right and descends along the inside edge of the wood (later between fences) to the railway.

Cross over the railway (carefully). At the bottom cross over the busy A4010 (more dodgy than the railway). Continue across the field opposite, climbing gently to the top corner. The mausoleum and Golden Ball can be seen above the trees.

Turn left down the lane, following it round to the right past the entrance to the caves. Where the road bends left, continue straight on across the grass back to the start.

Inside the garden centre is an excellent tea room, an ideal way to finish the walk!

WALK 21 – STOKENCHURCH

DISTANCE:	**8km/5 miles**
TIME:	**2 hours**
MAP:	**OS Landranger 165, OS Explorer 171**
START:	**Car park by the King's Arms in Stokenchurch (Grid Ref 762963)**
REFRESHMENTS:	**The Crown, 'The City'; King's Arms and fish and chip shop, Stokenchurch**

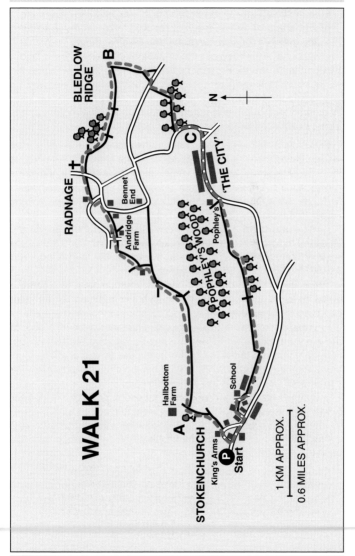

WALK 21

BLEDLOW RIDGE

B

RADNAGE

Bennet End

Andridge Farm

STOKENCHURCH

Hallbottom Farm

A

King's Arms

P

Start

School

POPHLEY'S WOOD

Pophley's

C

'THE CITY'

N

1 KM APPROX.
0.6 MILES APPROX.

One of the shorter walks in the book – nevertheless there are plenty of superb views en route. The walk explores the peaceful valley between Stokenchurch and the Bledlow Ridge.

START: The free public car park by the Kings Arms by the village green in Stokenchurch (grid ref 762963). Stokenchurch is reached by proceeding westwards from High Wycombe along the A40 past West Wycombe and Piddington before climbing the ridge. Regular buses from High Wycombe stop at Stokenchurch.

THE WALK: From the car park head northwards along the edge of the village green, passing the Kings Arms on the left. Turn left along a lane, then left along Park Lane. Ignore all turnings off. Soon the traffic noise from the A40 is left behind. **(A)** Ignore the drive to Hallbottom Farm, as the track heads eastwards along the ridge. Soon a view across to the Bledlow Ridge opens out.

Later turn left by a waymark arrow, then turn right immediately along the top edge of two fields (hedge on your right). Go down some steps, cross over the track and bear left across the field opposite to reach a track running along the valley bottom.

Turn right along this track. At a T-junction turn left along a metalled track. At a public footpath sign turn right across the field, climbing to a hedge gap in the top corner. Go to the left of a telegraph pole. Pass through the hedge gap, and turn right over a stile. At the top, turn right over a stile, crossing the drive to Andridge Farm. Fork right, passing to the left of the farmhouse. Ahead is a long view along the valley towards West Wycombe; the church and golden ball can be seen on the ridge-top to the left.

Continue straight on down the left-hand edge of the field. Bear left through a hedge gap in the field corner to reach a lane.

Turn left along this lane. At a T-junction turn left. Turn right across a long field towards Radnage church. Cross over a lane then continue up the drive to the church.

Radnage church dates from the 13th century, although it was enlarged in the 15th century. Its most prominent feature is the large central tower. The church itself is usually locked. There are attractive views across the fields from the churchyard.

Bear right through the churchyard, passing to the right of the church. Cross over the stile in the wall on the far side of the church-yard, and bear right across the field to a further stile. After crossing the next stile bear right to a stile by a gate in the corner of the field. Looking back there is a fine view across to Radnage church in its peaceful setting.

Continue straight on along the left-hand edge of two fields, ignoring two cross-paths. Later the path bears left (between fences) and climbs up to the Bledlow Ridge. **(B)** At the top turn right down a track. Turn right over some metal steps, steeply descending the field to a stile at the bottom.

Ahead is a panoramic view across towards Stokenchurch and the Telecom tower, one of the most prominent Chiltern landmarks.

Turn right along this lane, then left by a public footpath sign across the field to the wood ahead. Turn right, following the path through the wood, starting to climb later. Turn left along a lane, climbing back up to the Stokenchurch Ridge. **(C)** At the top turn right along City Road, passing the village school and the Crown pub.

'The City' is the largest of a group of settlements making up the parish of Radnage. It is a collection of cottages and more modern bungalows.

Turn right along the drive to Pophleys. Cross over a stile and continue straight on between fences. Cross the field to the right-hand end of the opposite hedge. Continue along a grassy track and along the ridge-top back towards Stokenchurch, seen ahead.

Later the track follows a hedge and a row of trees. At the end of the hedge continue straight on across the field. Follow the path between the fences, round the edge of a playing field.

At a kissing gate continue straight on. On reaching a road, turn right passing Stokenchurch County Middle School. Turn right along a tarmac footpath just after No 39. Turn left along a road, then right along the A40 back to the village green and the start.

Stokenchurch is a large village, the oldest part centered around a large triangular village green. The Kings Arms Hotel is a replica of the original 18th-century coaching inn. There is an old pub in the middle of the village green. Opposite the car park is a general stores and an excellent fish and chip shop in the parade next to the King's Arms.

WALK 22 – WEST WYCOMBE TO FINGEST

DISTANCE:	**16km/10 miles**
TIME:	**4 hours**
MAP:	**OS Landranger 175, OS Explorer 171/172**
START:	**Car park adjacent to West Wycombe garden centre (Grid Ref 826947)**
REFRESHMENTS:	**Brickmakers Inn, Wheeler End; Chequers, Fingest; Dashwood Arms, Piddington; West Wycombe**

Linking two of the most popular places in the Chilterns, West Wycombe and Fingest, this walk goes through woodlands to the heart of the Hambleden Valley, one of the most beautiful parts of Buckinghamshire.

START: The large car park alongside the garden centre in West Wycombe (grid ref 826947). It is reached from High Wycombe by taking the A40 westwards towards Stokenchurch. West Wycombe is at the end of the built-up area. Regular buses from High Wycombe stop at West Wycombe.

THE WALK: Turn right out of the car park, then turn right along the A40. Turn left up a straight lane, passing West Wycombe House on the left.

West Wycombe Park was acquired by the Dashwood family in 1698. The present house was built by Sir Francis Dashwood (as was the church and mausoleum on the hillside opposite). The house and park are now owned by the National Trust. The entrance to the house is through the South Front, a two-storey colonnade. From the hall, a staircase leads to the pillared gallery above. From the house there is a superb vista across to the Music Temple in the grounds, with the church and mausoleum behind. The Music Temple, in its lake setting, is the focal point of the grounds, where each summer one of the National Trust's popular firework concerts is held.

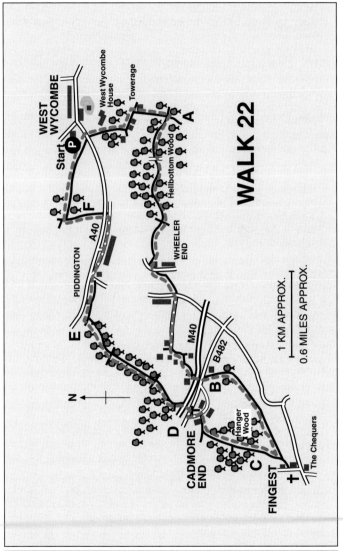

WALK 22

WEST WYCOMBE

West Wycombe House

Towerage

Start

P

F

A40

PIDDINGTON

Hellbottom Wood

WHEELER END

A

E

M40

B482

N

D

CADMORE END

Hanger Wood

C

FINGEST

The Chequers

1 KM APPROX.

0.6 MILES APPROX.

B

At the top the track bends left. Turn right by a white cottage and continue along the left-hand edge of the field ahead. Continue down between a hedge and fence to reach Hellbottom Wood.

(A) Turn right at a cross-paths (marked by a waymark post) in the middle of the wood. Follow the narrow (but fairly well-defined) path through the wood. Keep to the top edge of a clearing. Later the path swings right. Carry straight on over two cross-tracks (following a waymark post, then a waymark arrow on a tree).

Follow the right-hand side of a second clearing, then follow a series of waymark arrows through the wood. Keep parallel to the valley track. Later merge with a track. At the wood edge turn left at a T-junction, then right over a stile. Follow the right-hand edge of the field.

Cross over a stile in the field corner, then bear right to a further stile and continue to the edge of a barn. Turn left along a lane to reach Wheeler End Common.

Fork right along the edge of the common alongside some scrub on your left. Later bear right across the common to the war memorial. Cross the road and continue along the lane opposite (past Orchard Row). Continue straight on at Watercroft Farm. Ignore all turnings off. Later turn left at a T-junction. **(B)** At a cross-roads turn left to cross over the M40. Cross over the B482 and continue along the track opposite. At a cattle grid bear right across the field to a stile. The path passes between a hedge and fence, then continues down the right-hand edge of the field to reach a wood.

In the wood follow a narrow path straight on downhill (at first there are steps to help you). Ignore the wider path along the top edge of the wood. On leaving the wood bear right across the fields, following a series of stiles. Looking ahead there is your first glimpse of the glorious Hambleden Valley.

Continue along a track, later running alongside the southern edge of Hanger Wood. Where the track bends left continue straight on alongside a fence on your left to reach the village of Fingest. Turn left past the church to reach the Chequers pub.

Fingest is one of the prettiest villages, set in a deep wooded valley. Somehow the valley sides are steeper here than further north in the Chilterns. St. Bartholomew's church has a large tower which seems out of proportion to the tiny nave. The twin gabled roof was added later. There were once eight bells in the tower, but several of them were lost to nearby Hambleden as a result of a card game between the two vicars!

Inside, the church is simple in style, though the south wall of the nave contains a stained-glass window depicting Psalm 150 'Praise him with the Lute & Harp, praise him with the trumpet and cymbals'.

On a notice board outside the church is an essay written by the late Sir William Connor ('Cassandra' of the Daily Mirror), who lived in Fingest. The piece shows how St. Bartholomew's church has its roots deep in English history. In the porch of the church are a couple of poems about the village.

Opposite the church is the Chequers pub – ideal for a lunch stop at about the halfway point. The pub is so named because, in the days before high-street banks, money changed hands in pubs which came to be called 'Chequers'.

In the nearby woods the ghost of a 14th-century bishop has occasionally been seen. He enclosed common land for the church's use, and his ghost, dressed as a forester, is doomed for ever to wander penitently for his crimes.

(C) Retrace your steps out of the village. Bear left between fences to climb up to Hanger Wood. Just before entering the wood, looking back there is a superb view of Fingest in its position at the head of the Hambleden Valley. Follow the path through the wood, ignoring a footpath going off to the left. This path is called Church Path as it links the church of St. Bartholomew, Fingest, with that of St. Mary-Le Moor, Cadmore End.

At the top of a rise, after leaving the wood the track bends right to reach Cadmore End.

Cadmore End is a linear village along the ridge between Stokenchurch and Marlow. It is a collection of cottages on the edge of a series of commons.

Turn left along the road past the church. (D) Turn right along the edge of the green, after the last cottage, to reach the B482. Turn right along the road, then left at a public footpath sign to pass underneath the M40. Fork right by a yellow waymark to rejoin the track at the bottom. Turn right along this track, ignoring all turnings off. Later fork right (by a waymark arrow) through a forest gate. Continue straight on over two cross-tracks along a strip of woodland. Ignore a path going off to the right just before leaving the woods.

(E) On leaving the woods, turn right at a T-junction (hedge on the right). Continue along a track to reach Piddington. Turn left along the road, then right along the slip road (parallel to the A40) past the Dashwood Arms. In just over half a mile (1km) (passing the houses) turn left. **(F)** Cross over the A40 and continue up the track opposite. Near the top turn right into the wood by a waymark arrow. Follow the narrow path through the wood. There are white marks on the trees either side of the path to guide you. On leaving the wood continue straight on alongside a fence on your left.

The effort made in this final climb is rewarded by one of the finest views in this part of the Chilterns – a vista down to West Wycombe ahead, with the church and mausoleum on the left and West Wycombe Park on the right. Shame about the telegraph wire in the way further down the slope though!

Follow the path straight on down across two large fields to reach a squeeze-stile at the bottom. Turn left along the A40 retracing your steps back to the start.

WALK 23 – FINGEST, IBSTONE AND TURVILLE

DISTANCE:	**10km/6¼ miles**
TIME:	**3 hours**
MAP:	**OS Landranger 175, OS Explorer 171**
START:	**Village of Fingest (Grid Ref 777912)**
REFRESHMENTS:	**Chequers, Fingest; The Fox, Ibstone;**
	Bull and Butcher, Turville

This walk takes you into the heart of the Chilterns, with deep valleys, beechwoods and the prettiest of villages. Starting in

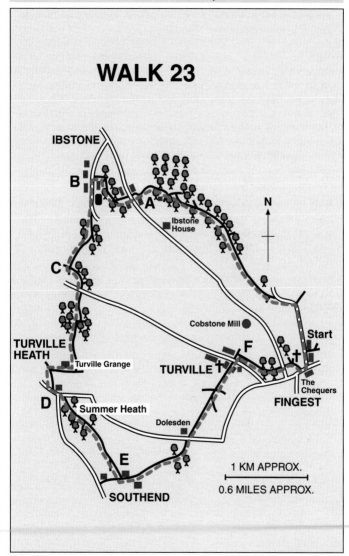

WALK 23

IBSTONE

B

A

Ibstone House

N

C

Cobstone Mill

Start

TURVILLE HEATH

Turville Grange

F

TURVILLE

D

Summer Heath

The Chequers

FINGEST

Dolesden

E

1 KM APPROX.

0.6 MILES APPROX.

SOUTHEND

Fingest, it visits the ridge-top villages of Ibstone and Turville Heath before returning to Turville.

START: The village of Fingest. Fingest is reached from High Wycombe by proceeding west along the A40 past West Wycombe to Piddington. Fingest is signposted from here, reached by country lanes. As you drop down from the ridge towards Fingest from the B482 you are greeted with a superb view as your first glimpse of the Hambleden Valley. There is limited parking in the lane by the church and the Chequers pub (grid ref 777912). Alternative parking is available in nearby Turville. A bus links High Wycombe with Ibstone.

THE WALK: From the church, head northwards along the lane (past a 'Single Track Road' sign). Where the lane bends right, turn left along a track by a metal gate. Keep to the track along the valley bottom.

On the ridge-top to the left is Ibstone House, once owned by the novelist Dame Rebecca West. The valley path is also a bridleway, but for some of the way there is an alternative path alongside.

Ignore tracks going off right, then left. **(A)** At a waymark post turn left along a bridlepath through some pines. Turn left along a track at a T-junction. Bear right up a small path by a yellow waymark arrow. On leaving the wood continue straight on across the field to a line of trees ahead. Cross over a stile and continue along the right-hand side of the field and on between fences to reach the village of Ibstone.

Ibstone is a scattered village, with its houses, built along two ridges, linked by a large common (and the Fox pub) at the northern end. The tiny church is at the southern end of the village overlooking the Turville Valley. The church contains a small wooded bell-turret instead of a tower. At the western end of the nave is a wooden gallery added around 1800. Red kites, which have recently been reintroduced to the Chilterns, are sometimes seen in the area.

Cross over the road and continue down the left-hand side of the field opposite. Turn right at a T-junction in the wood. Cross over a track in the valley bottom and continue straight on up the other side to a further part of Ibstone. **(B)** Turn left down the lane, passing some modern, but attractive, villas. At the end of the lane, carry straight on through a strip of woodland. Where the track bends left, bear right

Cottages at Turville, with the windmill visible on the hilltop, watching over the village

straight on downhill to emerge from the woods at the head of the Wormsley Valley. **(C)** Turn left along the drive at the bottom. Cross over the road and continue along the right-hand edge of the field opposite. Just before entering the wood, there is a fine view to the left along the valley towards Turville.

In the wood continue straight on over a track, climbing up towards Turville Heath. At first there are steps built into the hillside to help you. At the top of the steps turn right along a path which then turns left and continues to climb. On leaving the wood continue straight on across the field, later bearing left to pass alongside a fence on your right. Turn right over a stile on the far side of the field to pass Turville Grange.

The 18th-century Turville Grange is one of two big houses in Turville Heath, a number of houses situated around a large common.

Pass through a gate and turn left along the edge of the common. Turn left along a lane. **(D)** Just after the lane to Southend (another hamlet of cottages around a common) bear right into the woods, passing a public footpath sign just after entering the wood. Fork right (by a waymark arrow). Turn right along a track for a few paces, then fork left. There are intermittent waymark arrows to guide you.

On leaving the wood bear right across the field to a further stile, then continue alongside a fence on your right. By an oak tree bear left across the field to reach a stile (by a public footpath sign). **(E)** Turn left along the drive, then straight on along by a fence on your right. The path has been given a hard surface. Continue down through a spinney and on down to a lane at Dolesden.

Continue straight on over the road alongside a fence (on your left). On the far side continue down a path between fences to reach the village of Turville.

Turville is one of the most photographed places in the Chilterns. Its tiny village green is surrounded by some cottages, the Bull and Butcher pub and the village church. Like other churches in Buckinghamshire, St. Mary's church was restored in Victorian times, although the interior has remained unchanged since the 14th century. When the church was being restored, a tomb was found containing the remains of a 13th-century vicar, with a mysterious woman by his side with a bullet hole in her skull (the woman's remains, however, were from about 300 years later). A recent addition to the interior is a small stained-glass window by John Piper which commemorates St. Saviour's Chapel at Turville Heath, which was closed and converted to a house in the early 1970s.

The Bull and Butcher pub was opened around the time that the workmen restoring the church went on strike and refused to continue working until some liquid refreshment was provided. A villager quickly obtained a licence and opened the pub. On the ridge above the village is a smock mill, now converted into a house. The mill was featured in the film 'Chitty Chitty Bang Bang' as the inventor's home.

Continue along a track between cottages, leading towards the windmill. **(F)** Turn right through a kissing gate, bearing left across the field to a stile. Continue straight on along a terrace path through some scrub, crossing a lane. Turn right at a cross-paths to return to Fingest (see Walk 22 for details of the village). Bear left across the church-yard back to the parked car.

Opposite the church is the Chequers Inn – ideal for a drink and meal at the end of the day. The pub is so named because, in the days before high-street banks, money changed hands in pubs which came to be known as 'Chequers'. The word 'cheque' comes from this custom.

WALK 24 – HAMBLEDEN TO SKIRMETT

DISTANCE:	**11km/7 miles**
TIME:	**3 hours**
MAP:	**OS Landranger 175, OS Explorer 171**
START:	**Public car park in Hambleden (Grid Ref 785866)**
REFRESHMENTS:	**Walnut Tree, Fawley (short detour); The Frog, Skirmett; Stag and Huntsman, Hambleden; shop, Hambleden**

Hambleden is the definitive English village, and has featured in various television programmes. The backdrop to the village is the wooded slope on either side of the valley. The walk takes in the beechwoods to the west of the village and the Chilterns' own vineyard before descending to Skirmett and returning along the valley.

START: The public car park in the village of Hambleden at the back of the Stag and Huntsman pub (grid ref 785866). Hambleden is reached from High Wycombe by following the directions to Fingest (signposted along country lanes from Piddington on the A40), then continuing southwards along the Hambleden Valley road. Buses from Marlow and Henley stop at Greenlands (grid ref 776855), where the walk can be joined.

THE WALK: From the car park, turn left to reach the village centre.

The historic village of Hambleden is now protected by the National Trust. St. Mary's church dates from the 11th century and was enlarged in the 13th century. The tower was rebuilt in 1721, with its four corner turrets added in 1883. Inside is the D'Oyley monument, featuring Sir Cope D'Oyley, his wife and

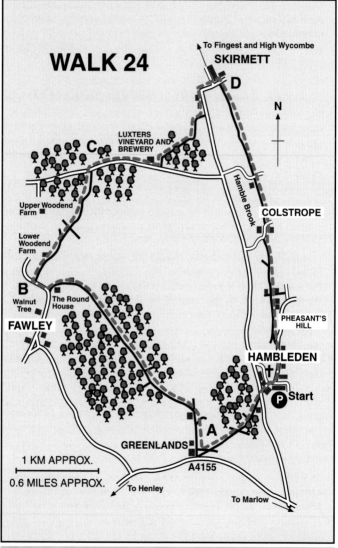

WALK 24

To Fingest and High Wycombe

SKIRMETT

D

N

LUXTERS
VINEYARD AND
BREWERY

C

Hamble Brook

COLSTROPE

Upper Woodend
Farm

Lower
Woodend
Farm

B

Walnut
Tree

The Round
House

FAWLEY

PHEASANT'S
HILL

HAMBLEDEN

P Start

A

GREENLANDS

A4155

1 KM APPROX.

0.6 MILES APPROX.

To Henley

To Marlow

their children. The children holding skulls died before their parents. In the churchyard is the 18th-century Kenrick mausoleum.

The Hamble Brook flows through the village, and around the village square are brick and flint cottages, the pub, a garage and the village shop. An old water pump stands in front of the shop.

Turn left past the village shop. Cross over the main Hambleden Valley road and continue along the footpath opposite (passing the old village school) to enter Ridge Wood. Fork right by a waymark arrow, climbing to the top of the ridge. From the top of the ridge there is a superb view across the Thames Valley, looking towards Henley and Fawley.

Continue straight on down the other side, ignoring a path going off to the right along the top of the ridge. Cross over a track at the bottom to reach a kissing gate. Continue along the left-hand edge of the field. After crossing a further track (a permissive footpath), continue across the fields to a public footpath sign on the main road (public transport users start here). **(A)** Turn sharp right along a track, passing Greenlands.

Greenlands was once the home of the first Viscount Hambleden (W.H. Smith), who died in 1891. It is now part of Henley Management College.

After the last cottage turn left along a track. Later fork right, climbing up to Great Wood. Follow the track through the woods. It is the only public right of way through the woods, which are privately owned. There are intermittent waymark arrows to guide you. Ignore two tracks going off left, then right, keeping to the waymarked track. On leaving the wood continue straight on between a hedge and fence.

(B) Turn right along a lane (the village of Fawley and the Walnut Tree pub are ¼ mile along to the left). Turn right along the drive to Lower Woodend Farm.

To the left is a superb view across to Maidensgrove with Bosmore Farm in the foreground. Between Bosmore Farm and Maidensgrove is the superb ridge path south from Stonor.

Later the path continues along the right-hand edge of a field, passing a converted barn on the left. Bear left over a stile in the field corner (the fence is now on your left). Later turn right across the field to a stile in the opposite hedge (the path is usually well defined). Turn left for a few paces, then turn right over the stile opposite. Cross the field to the gate opposite. Bear left along the left-hand edge of the next field. In the field corner turn left over a stile. Follow the path through the woods to reach a quiet lane. **(C)** Turn right along this lane, passing Luxters Vineyard and Brewery.

The first vineyard was planted in 1982, and since the first harvest in 1984 the Chiltern Valley wines produced here have gained a reputation for quality, helped by the fact that the winery is one of the most modern in Europe. The bottling facilities, cellar and barrel store are housed in traditional farm buildings. Luxters produce a range of wines and a traditional farm-brewed real ale (also sold in the local pubs). The cellar shop is open until 6pm (5pm in winter) – worth a detour on your way home!

Turn left by a public footpath sign along the eastern edge of the vineyard. Bear right across a long field to a hedge gap by an old gate. Cross over a track and follow the path down through the wood. Ahead is a fine prospect of Skirmett, with the tower of Fingest church behind, with the wooded slopes as a backdrop.

At the bottom turn right along a track, then left to a stile ('No FP' on a tree ahead). The path follows a fence on the right. Later the path swings right (between fences) to reach the Hambleden Valley Road. Turn left along the road to reach Skirmett.

Skirmett is an attractive village along the main Hambleden Valley Road. The names of some of the houses indicate their former use, 'All Saints' and 'The Old Bakery' for example. The village boasts a fine pub, The Frog at Skirmett – ideal for a lunch stop before the final (level) stretch back along the valley bottom back to Hambleden. Beyond the village is the Cobstone Mill on the hillside above Turville.

Continue straight on along the lane signposted to Freith and Lane End. **(D)** Turn right over a stile by a public footpath sign. Pass to the left of a line of trees ahead to reach a stile in the field corner. Continue along the right-hand edge of the next field. Bear left across a crossing track to a stile and continue along the left-hand edge of the next field.

Carry straight on across the next two fields (passing to the right of an oak tree).

Cross over a lane and continue straight on along a track between hedges (later between fields) to reach a lane at Colstrope. Where the lane bends right turn left through a kissing gate. Continue straight on between fences, then along by a hedge on your right (later left).

Continue straight on across a drive (by a multiple public footpath sign). The path passes through some cottage gardens. At a hedge corner continue straight on across the field to a stile in the line of pines ahead. Continue straight on across the fields, and Hambleden church is seen ahead. In the second field bear left to a kissing gate. Turn right along the lane back to the start, passing the churchyard and the Kenrick mausoleum.

WALK 25 – HAMBLEDEN TO MARLOW

DISTANCE:	**15km/9½ miles**
TIME:	**4 hours**
MAP:	**OS Landranger 175, OS Explorer 171/172**
START:	**Public car park in Hambleden (Grid Ref 785866)**
REFRESHMENTS:	**Hare and Hounds, Marlow; Stag and Huntsman, Hambleden; shop, Hambleden**

This is a walk of two halves, starting from Hambleden and proceeding through some of the Chiltern woodlands to the outskirts of Marlow, then returning alongside the Thames.

START: The public car park behind the Stag and Huntsman pub in Hambleden (grid ref 785866). Hambleden is reached from High Wycombe by proceeding along the A40 to Piddington, then following signs to Fingest (along country lanes), then continuing down along the main Hambleden Valley Road. Hambleden is also signposted

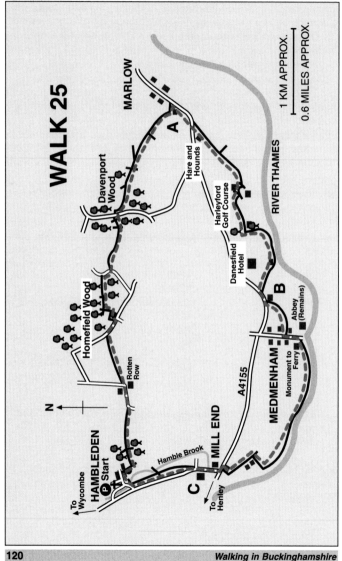

from Mill End on the main A4155 Henley to Marlow road. Buses from Henley and Marlow stop near the Hare and Hounds pub at the eastern end of the walk, and also at Mill End, at the foot of the Hambleden Valley.

THE WALK: Turn right out of the car park, then turn right along the first track, passing the playing fields on your right. At the end of the gardens on your left, turn left along a path between a fence and a hedge, soon climbing steeply out of the Hambleden Valley. Looking back just before entering the woods is a fine view across the southern end of the Hambleden Valley towards the River Thames.

Near the top continue straight on over a track, then bear right to a stile at the wood edge. Continue straight on across the field (the path is usualy well marked) to a gate. Head towards the left of a solitary tree (and to the right of the hedge ahead). Cross over a track and continue straight on between fields. Turn left along a lane to reach the hamlet of Rotten Row. Pass through a gate and continue across a large field to a stile ahead, then carry straight on across the next field. Turn right along a lane along the top edge of Homefield Wood. Ignore the first public footpath sign, then turn left at a cross-tracks (the public footpath sign is hidden in the hedge). The path passes round to the left of a house and garden, then swings left straight on downhill to a stile and onto the forestry track at the bottom. There are intermittent waymark arrows to guide you. Turn right along this track.

On leaving the wood turn right along a lane. Where the lane bends round to the left and starts to climb, turn left by a public footpath sign, along the right-hand edge of a couple of fields. The path then bears right between fences.

Continue straight on over a track at the wood edge, climbing steeply up through Davenport Wood. Bear left over a crossing path at the top to reach a lane (by a double public footpath sign). Continue straight on over this lane, past a Woodland Trust notice. Soon after, the path swings right by a waymark arrow on a tree (bank on the left). Follow the path through the wood – there are intermittent waymark arrows to guide you.

At a cross-paths, continue straight on, then turn right at a T-junction to reach the wood edge. Here, continue straight on along by a fence on your left. After passing through a second squeeze-stile bear right over a stile. Pass to the right of a waymark post. Ahead is Quarry

Wood, on the Berkshire side of the Thames. Continue straight on at a field corner (ignore a public footpath sign and a metal step-stile). Cross over a stile in the field corner and continue between fences.

Turn left through a kissing gate, and continue along a drive to reach the main A4155. Turn left here to explore the attractive country town of Marlow.

The popular town of Marlow is set between the chalk hills and the Thames. The town centre contains some attractive 17th- and 18th- century buildings, and the High Street leading down to the river has an elegant air about it (as well as some individual shops). By the river is the 19th-century All Saints' church. The suspension bridge was built by W.T. Clark (who also built the main bridge in Budapest) and offers fine views up and down the river.

(A) To continue the walk, turn right along the A4155 towards the excellent Hare and Hounds pub – ideal for a lunch break before returning to Hambleden along by the river.

Bear left along the public byway opposite the pub. Where the track bends left continue straight on over a stile, then along the right-hand edge of a series of fields. At the end of the fields, bear right uphill to reach a drive. The path is well marked at this point, where it passes through the recently created Harleyford Golf Club. Continue straight on over this drive, then bear right up some steps (between a wall and fence). Continue straight on over a second drive; the path bends right, then left along the edge of the golf couse. Later the path passes through some woods.

Turn left at a T-junction, passing through a tunnel. Follow the path along the river bank, below the grounds of the luxury Danesfield Hotel. Later the path joins a drive. Turn left along the main road for a few paces before turning left at a public footpath sign.

(B) Just before the house, turn right by some iron railings, then bear left through a spinney to reach a stile. Continue straight on across the field to a stile and on across the next field. The path then bends right between fences to reach the village of Medmenham.

Medmenham is a village of large houses along a lane leading south from the main road down to the Thames. The end of the lane is the site of the old Medmenham ferry and the remains of

Medmenham Abbey. After the Dissolution a house was built around the ruins of the abbey. In the 18th century the house was extended in Gothic style when it was rented by Sir Francis Dashwood. Early meetings of the Hell Fire Club were held here before the club relocated to West Wycombe.

Turn left down the lane. At the bottom turn right along the Thames towpath, passing the monument to the Medmenham ferry (and the ruins of Medmenham Abbey to the left). Later the impressive Culham Court, with its gardens reaching down to the river on the Berkshire Bank is passed. To the right is a vista along the length of the Hambleden Valley, with the Cobstone Mill above Turville at the head.

Further on turn left over a stile and continue along a drive to reach the main road at Mill End. **(C)** Turn left along the main road, then right along the Hambleden Valley road (signposted to Hambleden). A short detour here brings you to the photogenic Hambleden Mill (now converted into luxury apartments) and weir, complete with a foot-bridge across the river.

At the lane signposted to Rotten Row, bear right through a kissing gate, crossing the fields parallel to the Hambleden Valley Road. Cross a track via a couple of kissing gates and continue across the next field. The village of Hambleden, with its cathedral-like church, is seen ahead. Turn right along the lane leading back to the village centre (past the village shop). Turn right, past the Stag and Huntsman, back to the start.

WALK 26 – LANE END TO MARLOW

DISTANCE:	**14km/9 miles**
TIME:	**4 hours**
MAP:	**OS Landranger 175, OS Explorer 172**
START:	**Public car park in Lane End (Grid Ref 807918)**
REFRESHMENTS:	**Royal Oak, Bovingdon Green**

Wide views and Chiltern beechwoods are the highlights of this

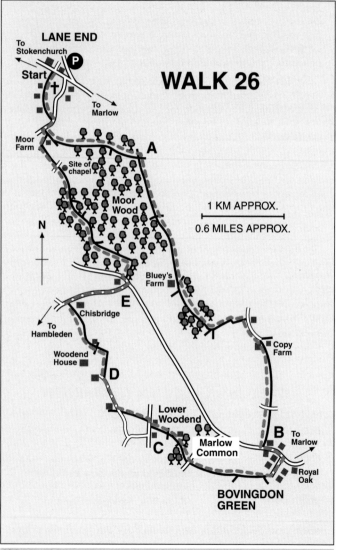

WALK 26

LANE END

To Stokenchurch

P

Start

To Marlow

Moor Farm

Site of chapel

A

Moor Wood

1 KM APPROX.

0.6 MILES APPROX.

N

Bluey's Farm

E

Chisbridge

To Hambleden

Copy Farm

Woodend House

D

Lower Woodend

B

To Marlow

C

Marlow Common

Royal Oak

BOVINGDON GREEN

walk linking Lane End, on the outskirts of High Wycombe, and Bovingdon Green, on the edge of Marlow.

START: The public car park in Lane End (grid ref 807918). Lane End is reached from High Wycombe centre by proceeding up Marlow Hill, then turning right at the top of the hill (before the main Handy Cross roundabout). Turn right towards Booker, and continue straight on at a roundabout. Turn right onto the B482 to reach the village. Buses from High Wycombe stop in the village.

THE WALK: From the car park, cross over the B482 along the track towards the church. Pass to the right of the church and continue alongside a wall on your left.

Holy Trinity church was built in 1878 in a 13th-century style. The tower was enlarged and capped in 1901. Inside there is a long nave with lancet windows, a small transept and a small two-bay chancel chapel, although the church is usually locked.

Soon you emerge onto the large village green. Continue along a track, passing a forge works and some cottages on your right to reach a road. Turn right along this road. When the road bends right turn left along a drive, passing The Bungalow on your left. Later, bear left past the 17th-century Moor Farm House. Bear left over a stile by a public footpath sign. Cross the field to a stile in the opposite fence. In the next field bear left to a stile. Continue along the inside edge of the wood ahead. Follow a series of white-topped posts. Continue along the bottom edge of a field, sometimes used for scrambling. Turn left at a T-junction onto a track leading across Moor Wood. Ignore a track going off to the right uphill.

(A) Turn right at a cross-paths at the wood edge. Carry straight on over the next cross-paths. On leaving the wood continue along the right-hand edge of two fields, before bearing left to a bridlegate in the top corner of the second field. Looking back there is a fine view of Bluey's Farm in its peaceful wooded valley setting.

Turn right at a T-junction. Continue straight on over a track (between a hedge and fence). Turn left over a stile (with steps leading up to it) in the second field and follow the track across the wood. Ignore a footpath going off to the right. Turn left along a track, climbing to the top of the ridge. Turn right at a T-junction near the top. Turn right at the top along a lane past a solitary cottage. At the end of the lane continue straight on across the farmyard to a gate, then across the field to a second gate. Ahead is a fine view across to Marlow.

Follow a faint track down the ridge. Later bear left to the field edge. At the bottom cross over the lane and continue up the other side. **(B)** At the top turn left along a lane to reach Bovingdon Green.

Bovingdon Green consists of a number of houses around a large village green just off the main road. It has now become a suburb of Marlow. The village has a fine pub, the Royal Oak, with a selection of reasonably priced bar food and a friendly labrador!

Turn right along the lane signposted 'Bovingdon Green'. At the end turn right along a track. Ignore a public footpath going off to the left and continue between fences.

Bear right over a stile. Follow the waymark arrows across two fields and on between fences. Cross over a lane, and carry straight on at a cross-tracks. Turn left at a T-junction and continue straight on over a track (between fences).

(C) On leaving the wood bear right down the field to a stile in front of a barn in the valley and up the other side (hedge on right). At the top, continue between fences. Turn right along a lane. Turn left across the field just before the lane starts to descend. Make for a stile in the opposite fence (with a public footpath sign) in front of a cottage ahead.

Turn right along a second lane. There are fine views left and right.

(D) At the end of the lane continue along a grassy track, then along the left-hand edge of a field. Turn left over a stile (fence on left). Carry straight on over a track, passing a barn on your right. To the left is Woodend House. At the fence corner bear right across the field to a stile (the path is faintly marked) then continue along by a fence on the right.

Turn right down a lane. At the bottom turn left. **(E)** Turn right along a narrow path by a public footpath sign just before the road bends left and the main track leading off into the (private) woods. BEWARE: The path is easy to miss, especially in the height of summer.

At the top of the rise the path turns left into the wood. Follow the track through the woods (intermittent white-topped posts). Later the track bears right at a wood corner (at a cross-tracks). Where the track bends right and descends to the valley bottom, continue straight on along a narrower path, past a waymark arrow on your right. Turn left at a T-junction and leave the wood at a stile. Cross the corner of the field to a stile in the opposite fence. Cross over this stile and turn left along by a fence (on your left). The spinney on the right is the site of Ackhampstead Chapel, which was demolished in 1849.

Cross over a track and across a large field to a white kissing gate in the opposite fence. Follow the path through the trees. Turn right at a T-junction (by a wall on your right). After passing some cottages, you reach the drive to Moor Farm. Turn right along the road, retracing your steps back to the start.

WALK 27 – WOOBURN

DISTANCE:	**8km/5 miles**
TIME:	**2 hours**
MAP:	**OS Landranger 175, OS Explorer 172**
START:	**Parish car park behind Wooburn church (Grid Ref 911878)**
REFRESHMENTS:	**Jolly Woodman, Littleworth Common**

This introduction to the landscape of south Buckinghamshire is more of a gentle stroll, as the walk is more or less level after the initial climb out of the Wye Valley.

START: The parish car park behind the church in Wooburn, facing the playing fields (grid ref 911878). Wooburn is reached from Beaconsfield by proceeding west along the A40, then turning left along the B4440 (later the A4094) down to the Wye Valley. Turn left just before the church (after passing the playing fields) and the car park is on the left. Buses from Wycombe stop in Wooburn.

THE WALK: From the car park turn right along the edge of the recreation ground. Fork right onto a narrower path, starting to climb. At a stile in the field corner turn left over a second stile across a large field (signposted to Bergers Hill).

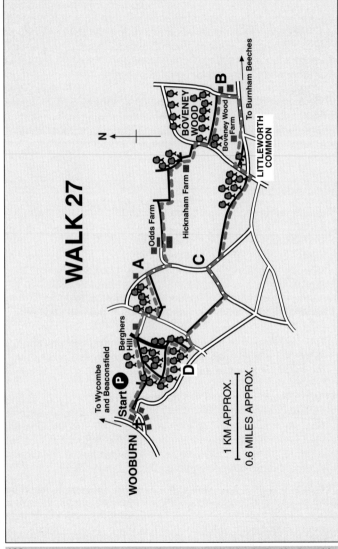

WALK 27

The remains of Medmenham Abbey, now part of a house (Walk 25)

Culham Court, overlooking the Thames near Medmenham (Walk 25)

The Chinese Gazebo in the Water Garden at Cliveden (Walk 28)

Looking back, there is a fine view of Wooburn in its Wye Valley setting, although the view is somewhat marred by the telegraph wires. Wooburn church dates from medieval times, although it was restored in the 1860s. However, the church is usually locked. The view of the valley is dominated by the tall chimney of a Victorian paper mill.

Continue straight on through the wood (fence on the left). At the top continue straight on between cottages, then on along a lane past some large houses. At the end turn right along the road. Turn left by a public footpath sign along the inside edge of the woods (between a fence and ditch). **(A)** Turn right along the road at the end of this path, then left along a track just after the drive to Odds Farm.

Odds Farm keeps some rare breeds of farm animals. The farm is open to the public at certain times and holds a daily programme of 'hands on' activities, such as bottle-feeding lambs, and goat and cow milking, together with tractor and trailer rides, and weekend 'theme events'.

Bear left through the caravan park and continue along a path on the far side (by a public footpath sign). Continue through two kissing gates along the left-hand edge of the field. Turn right at a T-junction (hedge on the right). Later the path bends left to reach a track. Turn right along this track. Turn right at a five-point junction, passing to the left of some farm buildings. At the end of the track bear right, passing to the right of a spinney to reach the road. Turn right along this road, then left over a stile (by a public footpath sign). Follow this path across Boveney Wood. **(B)** At the end of the path turn right along a quiet lane, then right at a T-junction. Just after Common Lane bear right along a path by a public bridleway sign. Carry straight on past some cottages to reach the hamlet of Dropmore, part of Littleworth Common. Turn left along a road by the Jolly Woodman pub.

Littleworth Common/Dropmore is made up of a number of cottages, a pub (the Jolly Woodman) and a tiny church in clearings of the beechwood. The church was built in 1866, with the transept added in 1877. The west gable is timber framed and painted blue, and the bell turret also is made of wood. The church is usually closed. Opposite the church is the village hall.

Turn right by a public footpath sign onto the Beeches Way, a recreational path across South Buckinghamshire. At the end of the wood bear left across a large field in the direction of a waymark arrow to the hedge corner ahead, then on over a stile.

(C) Turn right along Wooburn Common Road, then left down Sheepcote Lane. Turn right along a track by a public bridleway sign. Turn left along the road at the end of this path. **(D)** Where the road bends left, turn sharp right along the bridleway signposted to Mill Wood. At the entrance is an information board giving details of the various flowers found in these woods throughout the year.

Where the track bends right, bear left into the woods along a public footpath (yellow waymarks). Fork left downhill. Turn right at a cross-tracks in a dip along the inside edge of the wood. At a T-junction turn left across a large field, rejoining the outward route. Retrace your steps back to the start.

WALK 28 – CLIVEDEN

DISTANCE:	**5km/3 miles**
TIME:	**2 hours**
MAP:	**OS Landranger 175, OS Explorer 172**
START:	**National Trust car park, Cliveden**
REFRESHMENTS:	**National Trust restaurant, Cliveden;**
	Feathers pub (by entrance to Cliveden)

Like the walk round the gardens of Stowe in North Buckinghamshire (Walk 3), this is a stroll around the woodland gardens of Cliveden, now owned by the National Trust. The walk starts in the formal gardens near the house before descending to the Thames and returning through woodland to the famous water gardens.

START: The National Trust car park at the north end of the estate. The entrance to the grounds is opposite the Feathers pub. Cliveden is reached from Junction 2 of the M40 by proceeding down the A355 towards Slough for about quarter of a mile (.5km), then turning right towards Littleworth Common. Turn right by the village school, then

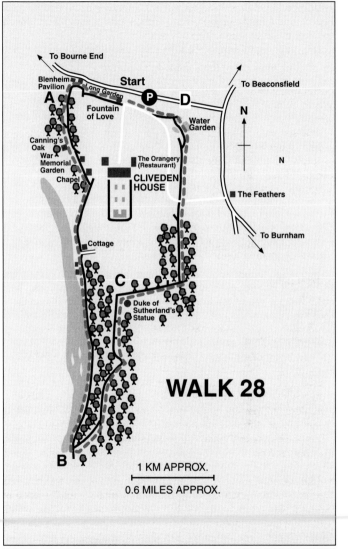

To Bourne End

Blenheim
Pavilion

Long Garden

Start

P

D

To Beaconsfield

N

N

A

Fountain
of Love

Water
Garden

Canning's
Oak

War
Memorial
Garden

Chapel

The Orangery
(Restaurant)

**CLIVEDEN
HOUSE**

The Feathers

To Burnham

Cottage

C

Duke of
Sutherland's
Statue

WALK 28

B

1 KM APPROX.

0.6 MILES APPROX.

left down Heathfield Road to reach the Feathers pub. Entrance for non-National Trust members is £5. The gardens are open from March to December.

THE WALK: Turn right out of the car park towards the Fountain of Love at the head of the drive towards the house.

The house was built by Sir Charles Barry in the 19th century, the third house on the site. The owner of the first house, the second Duke of Buckingham, had the grand terrace in front of the house built, along with the parterre. The Astor family lived in the house from 1893 to 1966. In the early 1960s, Lord Astor was involved in the Profumo affair when it was alleged that he gave financial assistance to Christine Keeler and Mandy Rice-Davies, along with Stephen Ward, who rented a cottage on the estate. Among Christine Keeler's 'clients' were Jack Profumo (then a government minister) and Captain Eugene Ivanhof, the Soviet naval attaché. Profumo was forced to resign when it was revealed that he had shared a call girl with a Russian, as it was feared that he might have given away top secret information.

Continue straight on along the green ride opposite. On the right is the Long Garden with several fine examples of topiary. **(A)** Turn right along a gravel track, round by the Blenheim Pavillion. Later Canning's Oak is reached. The statesman is said to have spent many hours admiring the view down to the Thames, perhaps pondering over political issues of the day!

Fork right, past the War Memorial Garden. Later the path passes beneath the Octagon Temple.

The temple was a gazebo which was converted into a chapel in 1893. The chapel is open on Thursday and Sunday afternoons, when the garden is open.

Turn right down the stepped path to the river. The steps are made from the yew trees of the estate which were salvaged after being blown down in the gales of 1987 and 1990. At the bottom continue straight on past a boathouse and cottage. Ignore two paths going straight up the slope to the left. **(B)** Where the path bears left away from the river, turn sharp left along a track (past a National Trust Cliveden Reach notice). At the top turn left at a T-junction heedless of all turnings off.

The Fountain of Love at the head of the main drive at Cliveden

To the left is a superb view across the Thames Valley to Widebrook Moor, Cookham and Cookham Dean. **(C)** Later the path swings right by a statue of the Duke of Sutherland. From the statue is a superb vista across to the house, with the formal parterre in front.

Continue straight on over a cross-tracks. Soon after turn left along a wider track. Cross over the drive (leading to the car park). **(D)** Just before the track bends left, turn right (past a 'No Dogs' sign) then bear left along the edge of the lawn to reach the famous Water Garden. Bear left along a gravelled path, then turn right towards the Chinese Gazebo. The ponds in the Water Garden contain some fine carp (large goldfish).

After passing the Chinese Gazebo turn left at a T-junction on the far side of the Water Garden. This leads back to the car park.

The restaurant is located on the eastern side of the house and is open from Wednesday to Sunday and Bank Holiday Monday. The menu includes a wide range of vegetarian meals, and the excellent National Trust teas!

WALK 29 – BOVENEY AND DORNEY

DISTANCE:	**9km/5½ miles**
TIME:	**2 hours**
MAP:	**OS Landranger 175**
START:	**Car park near Boveney Court (Grid Ref 938778)**
REFRESHMENTS:	**None**

This is a gentle stroll by the River Thames, all level and on firm paths. Ideal for a hot summer's day.

START: The car park near Boveney Court (grid ref 938778). Boveney is reached from Junction 7 of the M4 by turning left off the motorway along the A4 towards Maidenhead, then turning left onto the B3026 to reach the village of Dorney. On the far side of the village turn right down a lane across Dorney Common to reach Boveney. The car park is at the end of this lane. Buses from Slough and Maidenhead stop in Dorney (no service on Sundays).

THE WALK: Turn left out of the car park along the lane back across Dorney Common, then turn left along the B3026 through the village.

Dorney has retained its character due to the influence of the Palmers (owners of Dorney Court) and Eton College, and Green Belt controls. Dorney Court was built in 1500 and has been in the ownership of the Palmer family since 1629. The Great Hall contains a selection of paintings of twelve generations of the family.

The first pineapple grown in England was given to Charles II at Dorney, an event commemorated by the Pineapple inn in the village. The name Dorney comes from the Saxon 'Isle of Bees,' and today the village is still famous for its honey. The villagers have had the right to rear cattle on Dorney Common since feudal times.

(A) Where the main road bends right, turn left along the road signposted to Dorney Reach, past Dorney Court. Where the road

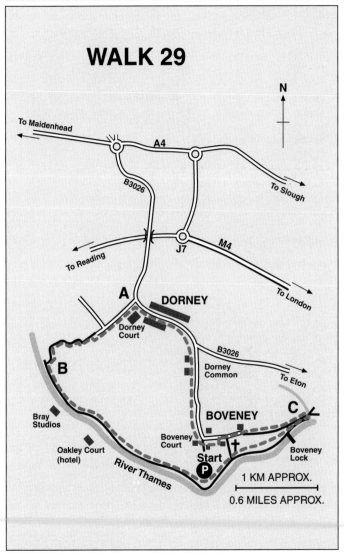

WALK 29

N

To Maidenhead

A4

To Slough

B3026

To Reading

J7

M4

To London

A

DORNEY

Dorney
Court

B3026

B

Dorney
Common

To Eton

Bray
Studios

BOVENEY

C

Oakley Court
(hotel)

Boveney
Court

Boveney
Lock

Start
P

River Thames

1 KM APPROX.

0.6 MILES APPROX.

Boveney church, a tiny riverside building reached by a footpath from the village

swings right, carry straight on along a recently made footpath (on the right of a new private road). This path winds its way across the fields to reach the Thames towpath. **(B)** Turn left along by the river, following the towpath for 2 miles (3.5km).

This stretch of the Thames marks the southernmost boundary of Buckinghamshire. Soon, Bray Studios are passed on the Berkshire bank. This is where the Hammer Horror films were made, and the studios still resemble a castle. Further on is the superb Victorian Gothic Oakley Court, now converted into a hotel.

Back on the Buckinghamshire side, the chapel of St. Mary Magdalen, Boveney, is eventually passed, reached by a footpath from Boveney Court. It has a combined nave and chancel with a weatherboarded bell turret. However, the church is usually locked.

Later the walk passes Boveney Lock. **(C)** After a further ¼ mile, turn left by a public footpath sign, alongside a tributary on your right. Ahead there is a fine view across the water meadows towards Eton.

Turn left along a track back towards Boveney. At Boveney Lock the track bears right away from the river alongside an avenue of horse chestnut trees. The chapel of St. Mary Magdalen is seen across the fields to the left. The end of the track leads back to the hamlet of Boveney, the lane to Dorney and the car park.

WALK 30 – BLACK PARK AND LANGLEY PARK

DISTANCE:	**6km/4 miles**
TIME:	**2 hours**
MAP:	**OS Landranger 176**
START:	**Car park at Black Park (Grid Ref 005833)**
REFRESHMENTS:	**Black Park Visitor Centre**

Black Park and Langley Park are both owned by Buckinghamshire County Council, bought in 1944 to save this rural haven between Uxbridge and Slough from development. Black Park is popular on summer weekends, although, as with other beauty spots, once away from the car park and lake the crowds seem to disappear. Much of the walk is on permissive paths, rather than definitive rights of way, so be aware that rights of access can be withdrawn or the route altered at any time. Along the walk there are detailed large-scale maps on notice boards and attached to trees.

START: The car park at Black Park (grid ref 005833). There is now a parking fee payable (pay and display). Black Park is reached from the A40 roundabout at Denham (the start of the M40) by taking the A412 towards Slough, then turning right along a road signposted to Stoke Poges and Wexham Street to reach the car park. The car park is closed at night. Buses from Langley and Slough stop at George Green, near the southwestern corner of the walk.

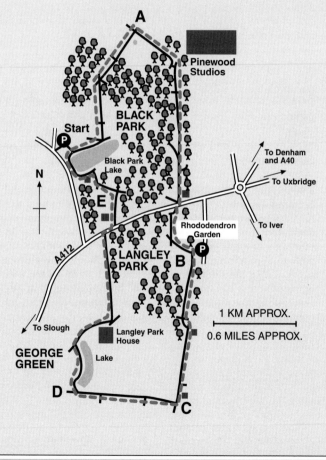

WALK 30

A

Pinewood
Studios

**BLACK
PARK**

Start

Black Park
Lake

N

E

To Denham
and A40

To Uxbridge

To Iver

Rhododendron
Garden

A412

**LANGLEY
PARK**

B

1 KM APPROX.

0.6 MILES APPROX.

To Slough

Langley Park
House

**GEORGE
GREEN**

Lake

D

C

THE WALK: From the car park head down a metalled path to the lake. Turn left along the lakeside path. At a cross-paths continue straight on along Queen's Drive, At a six-point junction bear right (northeast), rising gently. Continue straight on over cross-tracks.

On your left is a patch of heathland that has recently been regenerated by the Colne Valley Groundwork Trust. Later a drainage ditch and pond are reached. These ponds and ditches are a breeding ground for insects and amphibians. The ditches act as 'wildlife corridors', enabling these small creatures to pass around the park. They also are watering holes for larger creatures.

(A) Turn right down a track (across a cattle grid). Where the track bends right turn left at a cross-paths, then right at a T-junction.

On the other side of the fence are Pinewood Studios, where a number of films, including the classic 'Carry On' series, were made.

Continue straight on at a cross-paths, heedless of all turnings off. Later merge with a track coming in from the right. Cross the busy A412 and enter Langley Park via the public bridleway opposite. Turn left along a permissive path (the Beeches Way). Pass through the rhododendron garden heedless of all turnings off. Later bear left at a Beeches Way waymark (and a wooded sign directing you to the public toilets over to the right). The path passes the Langley Park yews (800 years old) and later there is a fine view across Langley Park. Turn right at a cross-paths. At a gate turn left along a track to reach the car park.

A couple of boards by the car park commemorate the naming of this path as the Rotary Jubilee Avenue of World Friendship, with the local Rotary Club joining up with similar organizations in Holland, Denmark, Australia, New Zealand, USA, India and Sri Lanka. One of the boards also quotes the following poem:

> *'You Know that you will never see*
> *A poem as lovely as a tree*
> *But poems are made by men like me*
> *And only God can make a tree'.*

(B) Turn right along the edge of the car park, and on down a track leading to the edge of the woods. Continue straight on over a cross-paths at the wood edge leading to a stile. Continue on between fences. Later ignore a path going off to the left. **(C)** At the end of the wall on the left turn right over a stile. Later pass through a kissing gate. **(D)** Turn right across the field on a permissive path (by a tree stump with a Langley Park map) to a concrete cairn, and on along by Langley Park lake.

Langley Park is an eighteenth-century mansion, built for the third Duke of Marlborough as a residence nearer to London than Blenheim Palace. The house is now an enviromental studies centre.

Turn right through a kissing gate along a drive to reach the front of the house. Turn left along the main drive, lined by an avenue of trees to reach the A412. Cross over the road again and turn right to re-enter Black Park. Turn left along a drive. **(E)** Turn left at a cross-tracks (by some picnic tables). At the next cross-tracks turn right to reach the lakeside. Turn left along the lakeside path round the southern end of the lake. After crossing a stream on the far side, turn left up a path returning to the car park.

WALK 31 – IVER

DISTANCE:	**6km/4 miles**
TIME:	**1 hour 30 mins**
MAP:	**OS Landranger 176**
START:	**Small car park by Iver library (Grid Ref 035812)**
REFRESHMENTS:	**Iver**

Iver has maintained its village character despite being close to Greater London. The walk explores the Slough Arm of the Grand Union Canal and part of the Colne Valley Park, the first stretch of open countryside reached on leaving London along the A40.

START: The small car park by the library in Iver (grid ref 035812). Iver is reached from Uxbridge by taking the A408 southwards towards

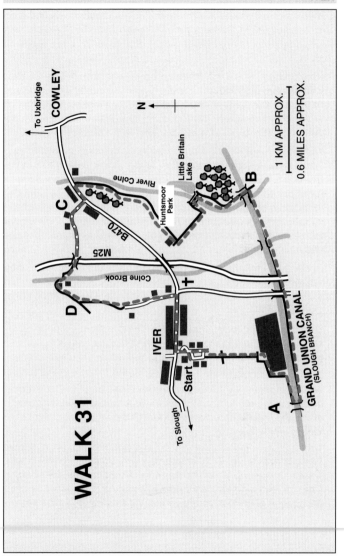

WALK 31

To Uxbridge
COWLEY

To Slough
IVER
Start

A

GRAND UNION CANAL
(SLOUGH BRANCH)

B

Little Britain
Lake

Huntsmoor
Park

River Colne

C

B470

M25

Colne Brook

D

N

1 KM APPROX.
0.6 MILES APPROX.

Cowley, then turning right onto the B470. The village is reached soon after crossing the M25. Buses from Uxbridge and Slough stop in Iver.

THE WALK: Turn left out of the car park. At the end of the road turn right, then left to a public footpath sign. Continue straight on across the field, crossing over a track (fence now on your right). Follow the path round the edge of an industrial estate (thankfully mostly hidden behind some trees). Later the path bends right, following a pylon line. Turn left over a bridge, crossing the canal. On the far side turn right down some steps to reach the canal towpath. **(A)** Turn right along the towpath.

The Slough Arm of the Grand Union Canal was completed in 1882, the last canal to be built in England. It was built to carry bricks from Slough to London. Later gravel was transported to London, and on the return journey the capital's refuse was carried to fill the gravel pits. Like the Grand Union and Kennet and Avon canals, the Slough Arm has received a new lease of life as a leisure spot. Herons are often seen by the canal, as are moorhens and mute swans.

Later pass beneath the M25. **(B)** At a small obelisk turn right, then left across a footbridge (now on the Colne Valley Way, a recreational path linking the River Thames at Staines with the Grand Union Canal at Uxbridge).

After passing beneath the M25 the canal crosses Colne Brook and the River Colne via a couple of aqueducts. In order to pacify the mill owners, the canal had to be built above the surrounding area so that it did not take water from these rivers.

The stone obelisk by the footbridge was a coal duty post, at which point coal bound for London was liable for duty. The River Colne marks the boundary between Buckinghamshire and Middlesex.

Later bear left between the Colne and Little Britain Lake. After crossing a footbridge turn left at a T-junction and continue along Ford Lane. Just before the M25 is reached turn right over a stile into Huntsmoor Park Farm. At the end of the concrete track continue straight on alongside a pretty riverside path through the woods to reach Iver Lane. **(C)** Turn left along this road (past some typical 1930s semi-detached surburban homes). Turn right along Palmers Moor Lane. Later fork right to cross over the M25.

The Slough Arm of the Grand Union Canal, completed in 1882

Fork right towards Deleford Manor Cottages. Cross over the River Colne and pass to the right of the cottages, and on between fences. **(D)** By a Beeches Way waymark, fork left over a stile along a path between fences.

Unfortunately the traffic noise from the M25 is always present along this stretch of the walk. However the path crosses a pretty meadow, full of buttercups in the spring. To the left is a view across the Colne Valley to Uxbridge.

After crossing a further stile turn left along a gravel track, which leads back to Iver village, coming out opposite the church.

The church of St. Peter, Iver, consists of an Anglo-Saxon nave, extended by adding a north aisle in the 12th century, with the tower, chancel and south aisle built in the 13th century. The north window is now the only part of the original Anglo-Saxon building remaining. The church is usually closed.

From the church, head west up Iver High Street back to the start.

WALK 32 – DENHAM AND THE GRAND UNION CANAL

DISTANCE:	13km/8 miles
TIME:	3 hours
MAP:	OS Landranger 176
START:	Colne Valley Park centre (Grid Ref 048865)
REFRESHMENTS:	Coy Carp and Horse and Barge (both along the canal); Denham Country Park visitors' centre and Colne Valley Park Centre

Starting from the pretty Denham village, the walk climbs out of the Colne Valley to part of the Old Shire Lane before returning along the Grand Union Canal. At times it is hard to believe that you are less than 20 miles from central London.

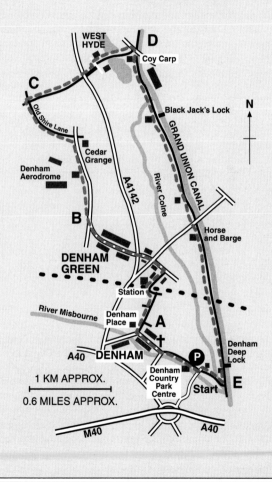

WALK 32

WEST HYDE

D

Coy Carp

C

Old Shire Lane

Black Jack's Lock

N

GRAND UNION CANAL

Cedar Grange

Denham Aerodrome

River Colne

A4142

B

Horse and Barge

DENHAM GREEN

Station

River Misbourne

Denham Place

A

Denham Deep Lock

A40 **DENHAM**

1 KM APPROX.

0.6 MILES APPROX.

Denham Country Park Centre

P

Start

E

M40   A40

START: The Colne Valley Park Centre (grid ref 048865). It is close to the A40. Coming from London, keep on the A40 at the start of the M40 and follow signs to Beaconsfield. The visitor centre is signposted from the first mini-roundabout. Trains from Marylebone to High Wycombe stop at Denham Station (on the route).

THE WALK: From the car park at Denham Country Park (pay and display) pass to the right of the visitor centre buildings to a kissing gate and the public footpath leading to Denham village. When the fence on your right ends, continue straight on across the golf course to a waymark post, then alongside a fence on your left, leading out to a minor road. Continue straight on along this road past the church and on through the village.

Denham is one of the prettiest villages in Buckinghamshire despite being close to Greater London. The village consists of a single street between the church and a tiny village green, with a bridge over the River Misbourne. Denham Place was built at the end of the 17th century, designed by William Stanton, a mason at Belton House, Lincolnshire.

St. Mary's church dates from the 13th century, although the tower may have Norman origins, as there are round-headed openings on either side of the belfry. The nave includes a brass monument to Sir Edmund Peckham, master of the Mint of Henry VIII, a monetarist who laid the foundations for the prosperity enjoyed during the reign of Elizabeth I. Also there are some pretty stained-glass windows. The church is open on Thursday lunchtimes and Sunday afternoons in the summer.

(A) Where the road bends left, continue straight on towards Denham Place, then turn right along a tarmac path. Ignore footpaths going off right, then left. Later the path bends left, then right to pass underneath the railway at Denham station. Continue straight on between a hedge and fence. Turn left along a minor road. Cross over a road to reach the A412. Cross this road and continue along Denham Green Lane, climbing out of the Colne Valley. **(B)** At the top turn right along Tilehouse Lane.

To the left is Denham aerodrome, with the runway close to the road. As you walk along this road, you are likely to encounter lightweight aircraft coming in to land over your head.

Later a picnic place is passed, followed by a caravan park (thankfully hidden from view). Just after Cedar Grange turn left along a public bridleway between fences (The Old Shire Lane). *Ahead is a fine view across the Colne Valley.* **(C)** Turn right at a cross-tracks in a dip (the South Bucks Way goes off to the left down to the Misbourne Valley at this point). Cross over the A412 and continue along the track opposite.

Turn left along a lane, then right almost immediately along the drive to West Hyde Nursery, and on between fences.

This path passes between two of the large lakes alongside the Grand Union Canal. In the 1940s and 1950s these were gravel pits, which were flooded when the quarrying finished. Some of the larger lakes have become nature reserves, as they attract a large bird and wildfowl population.

At a lane, bear slightly right to a stile and continue along a path between fences. Cross over the drive leading to the Clancy Group headquarters to reach the Coy Carp.

The Coy Carp is ideal for a lunch stop. It is open from 12am each day, and offers a varied menu and a wide range of wines.

(D) Turn right along a lane (leading to Harefield), then right along the canal towpath past the Coy Carp.

The Grand Union Canal was built between 1793 and 1805, and linked Braunston in Northamptonshire with the River Thames at Brentford. It was the M1 of its time, providing a direct route between London and Birmingham, carrying fleets of narrowboats and barges. There are still old mileposts remaining, giving the distance to Braunston along the towpath. Like other canals, the Grand Union lost out to the roads and railways, but since the 1950s it has become important for recreation and wildlife. The towpath provides varied canal scenes of locks, cottages, narrowboats and a wide range of wildlife all in peaceful surroundings.

Soon after joining the towpath some attractive, modern quayside houses are seen on the opposite bank. Bear left under the bridge at Black Jack's Lock. From this point the canal passes through open countryside.

Denham Deep Lock is the deepest lock on the Grand Union. The lock was made deep to take the canal over the Frays River, so that it did not disrupt the water power on which the mills in Uxbridge and Cowley depended.

(E) After passing Denham Lock turn right along a path (by a South Bucks Way waymark). This is the start of the South Bucks Way, a 22-mile path along the Misbourne Valley leading to the Hampden country and the Ridgeway at Coombe Hill. Cross over the River Colne. Pass through a kissing gate and cross Misbourne Meadows (by way of a gravel path alongside the fence on your right). Cross over a drive, then bear left back to the Colne Valley Park Centre.

FURTHER READING

The Buildings of England: Buckinghamshire, Nikolaus Pevsner (Penguin, 1960)

A Shell Guide – Buckinghamshire, Bruce Watkin (Faber and Faber, 1981)

England in Cameracolour – Buckinghamshire, John Bethell and Alan Hollingsworth (Town & Country Books, 1984)

Portrait of the Chilterns, Elizabeth Cull (Robert Hale, 1982); also includes the Vale of Aylesbury

National Trust guide books for Stowe Landscape Gardens, Claydon House, Hughenden Manor and Cliveden (all available at the properties)

The Churches of the Hambleden Valley (Wycombe District Council, 1999)

CICERONE GUIDES

THE MIDLANDS

CANAL WALKS Vol: 2 Midlands   *Dennis Needham*
  ISBN 1 85284 225 3 176pp

TWENTY COTSWOLD TOWNS   *Clive Holmes*
  Clive describes and draws the most interesting features of these attractive towns.
  ISBN 1 85284 249 0 144pp A4 Case bound

THE COTSWOLD WAY   *Kev Reynolds*
  A glorious walk of 102 miles along high scarp edges, through woodlands and magical villages by one of Britain's best guide writers.
  ISBN 1 85284 049 8 168pp

COTSWOLD WALKS (3 volumes)   *Clive Holmes*
  60 walks of between 1 and 10 miles, with local points of interest explained. Beautifully illustrated.
  ISBN 1 85284 139 7 (North) 144pp
  ISBN 1 85284 140 0 (Central) 160pp
  ISBN 1 85284 141 9 (South) 144pp

THE GRAND UNION CANAL WALK   *Clive Holmes*
  13 easy stages along the canal which links the Black Country to London. Delightful illustrations.
  ISBN 1 85284 206 7 128pp

AN OXBRIDGE WALK   *J.A. Lyons*
  Over 100 miles linking the university cities of Oxford and Cambridge. Generally undemanding and easy to follow.
  ISBN 1 85284 166 4 168pp

WALKING IN OXFORDSHIRE   *Leslie Tomlinson*
  36 walks from all parts of the county, and suitable for all the family.
  ISBN 1 85284 244 X 200pp

WALKING IN WARWICKSHIRE   *Brian Conduit*
  Attractive pastoral and gentle hill walks include Shakespeare country, the Avon and the Stour. Features many historic villages.
  ISBN 1 85284 255 5 136pp

WALKING IN WORCESTERSHIRE   *David Hunter*
  Part of the ever growing County Series, this book describes walks for all the family in Worcestershire.
  ISBN 1 85284 286 5 200pp 9

WEST MIDLANDS ROCK   *Doug Kerr*
  A guide to the popular crags.
  ISBN 1 85284 200 8 168pp

SOUTH AND SOUTH-WEST LONG DISTANCE TRAILS

THE KENNET & AVON WALK   *Ray Quinlan*
  90 miles along riverside and canal, from Westminster to Avonmouth, full of history, wildlife, delectable villages and pubs.
  ISBN 1 85284 090 0 200pp

THE LEA VALLEY WALK   *Leigh Hatts*

Split into 20 stages this 50 mile walk is one of the finest and most varied walking routes around the capital, tracing the route of the River Lea from the Millennium Dome to its source.
ISBN 1 85284 313 6 128pp)

THE NORTH DOWNS WAY and THE SOUTH DOWNS WAY   *Kev Reynolds*

Two major walks. The North Downs Way runs west from Farnham to Dover, while the South Downs way is a glorious easterly walk from Eastbourne. The routes are each split into 12 day sections, with advice on stopping points.

THE SOUTHERN COAST-TO-COAST WALK   *Ray Quinlan*

The equivalent of the popular northern walk. 283 miles from Weston-super-Mare to Dover.
ISBN 1 85284 117 6 200pp

SOUTH WEST WAY - A Walker's Guide to the Coast Path   *Martin Collins*
Vol.1: Minehead to Penzance
ISBN 1 85284 025 0 184pp PVC cover

Vol.2: Penzance to Poole
ISBN 1 85284 026 9 198pp PVC cover

Two volumes which cover the spectacular 560 mile coastal path around Britain's south-west peninsula. Profusely illustrated and filled with practical details.

THE THAMES PATH   *Leigh Hatts*

From the Thames Barrier to the source. This popular guide provides all the information needed to complete this delightful scenic route. 180 miles in 20 stages.
ISBN 1 85284 270 9 184pp

THE TWO MOORS WAY   *James Roberts*

100 miles crossing Dartmoor the delightful villages of central Devon and Exmoor to the rugged coast at Lynmouth.
ISBN 1 85284 159 1 100pp £5.99

THE WEALDWAY AND THE VANGUARD WAY   *Kev Reynolds*

Two long distance walks, from the outskirts of London to the south coast. The 81 mile Wealdway runs from Gravesend to Beachy Head, while the 62 mile Vanguard Way goes from Croydon to Seaford Head in Sussex.
ISBN 0 902363 85 9 160pp

SOUTHERN AND SOUTH-EAST ENGLAND

CANAL WALKS Vol 3: South   *Dennis Needham*
ISBN 1 85284 227 X 176pp

WALKING IN BEDFORDSHIRE   *Alan Castle*

32 fascinating walks of short and medium length for all abilities and interests. Maps and details of local interest abound.
ISBN 1 85284 312 8

WALKING IN THE CHILTERNS   *Duncan Unsworth*

35 short circular walks in this area of woods and little valleys with cosy pubs and old churches.
ISBN 1 85284 127 3 184pp

WALKING IN HAMPSHIRE   *David Foster and Nick Chandler*

With a range of landscapes from coastal beaches and marsh, downlands, river valleys and the New Forest, this county offers exceptional beauty. Delightful walks of short and medium length.
ISBN 1 85284 311 X

A WALKER'S GUIDE TO THE ISLE OF WIGHT   *Martin Collins & Norman Birch*
The best walks on this sunshine island, including short circuits and longer trails.
ISBN 1 85284 221 0 216 pp

WALKING IN KENT: Vol I   *Kev Reynolds*
ISBN 1 85284 192 3 200pp

WALKING IN KENT: Vol II   *Kev Reynolds*
ISBN 1 85284 156 7 200pp
Two books which cover the best of walking in the county.

LONDON THEME WALKS   *Frank Duerden*
Ten fascinating walks based on popular themes.
ISBN 1 85284 145 1 144pp

RURAL RIDES No.1: WEST SURREY
ISBN 1 85284 272 5 192pp

RURAL RIDES No.2: EAST SURREY
ISBN 1 85284 273 3 160pp   *Ron Strutt*

WALKING IN SUSSEX   *Kev Reynolds*
40 walks in the great variety of scenery and history of Sussex. Short walks and more demanding routes, including outline descriptions of some of the region's long distance paths.
ISBN 1 85284 292 X 240pp

SOUTH-WEST ENGLAND

CHANNEL ISLAND WALKS   *Paddy Dillon*
47 one-day walks in this wonderful holiday area, with easy bus and boat services. Walks on Jersey, Guernsey, Alderney, Sark and Herm.
ISBN 1 85284 288 1

CORNISH ROCK   *Rowland Edwards & Tim Dennell*
A superb photo topo guide to West Penwith, the most popular climbing in Cornwall, by the area's leading activists.
ISBN 1 85284 208 3 234pp A5 size Casebound

WALKING IN CORNWALL   *John Earle*
30 walks including the Coast Path and the interesting interior.
ISBN 1 85284 217 2 200pp

WALKING ON DARTMOOR   *John Earle*
The most comprehensive walking guide to the National Park. Includes 43 walks and outlines 4 longer walks.
ISBN 0 902363 84 0   224pp

WALKING IN DEVON   *David Woodthorpe*
16 coastal, 15 countryside and 14 Dartmoor walks.
ISBN 1 85284 223 7 200pp

WALKING IN DORSET   *James Roberts*
Circular walks between 5 and 12 miles in a rich variety of scene. Spectacular coastline, lovely downs and fine pubs.
ISBN 1 85284 180 X 232pp

A WALKER'S GUIDE TO THE PUBS OF DARTMOOR   *Chris Wilson & Michael Bennie*
60 Dartmoor inns. Everything a walker needs to know.
ISBN 1 85284 115 X 152 pp

EXMOOR AND THE QUANTOCKS *John Earle*
Walks for all the family on the moors, valleys and coastline.
ISBN 1 85284 083 8 200pp

WALKING IN THE ISLES OF SCILLY *Paddy Dillon*
With its mild climate and relaxing atmosphere, this is an ideal retreat. Walks and boat trips are described, with stunning scenery and beautiful plants and flowers.
ISBN 1 85284 310 1

WALKING IN SOMERSET *James Roberts*
Walks between 3 and 12 miles, gentle rambles to strenuous hikes, on Exmoor, the Quantocks and the pastoral lowlands.
ISBN 1 85284 253 9 280pp

NORTHERN ENGLAND LONG DISTANCE TRAILS

WALKING THE CLEVELAND WAY AND THE MISSING LINK *Malcolm Boyes*
Britain's 2nd LD path, the 115 mile circular tour of the North York Moors, including some of our finest coastline.
ISBN 1 85284 014 5 144pp

THE DALES WAY *Terry Marsh*
A practical handbook to a very popular walk. An ideal introduction to LD walking. Gentle, picturesque with accommodation guide.
ISBN 1 85284 102 8 136pp

THE ISLE OF MAN COASTAL PATH *Aileen Evans*
The coastline is of exceptional beauty. The Raad ny Foillan path encircles the island; the Herring Way and Millennium Way are also described.
ISBN 1 85284 277 6 152pp

THE ALTERNATIVE PENNINE WAY *Denis Brook & Phil Hinchliffe*
The APW goes from Ashbourne in Derbyshire to Jedburgh in the Borders, 431 km. Milder and more pleasant than the PW.
ISBN 1 85284 095 1 272pp

THE PENNINE WAY *Martin Collins*
By popular demand, Cicerone has produced a guide to the Pennine Way. Thoroughly researched by one of our most expert authors, this gives everything you need to know about Britain's first LD Trail.
ISBN 1 85284 262 8 144pp

THE ALTERNATIVE COAST TO COAST *Denis Brook & Phil Hinchliffe*
From Walney Island on the edge of the Lake District to Holy Island in Northumberland, across some of Britain's finest hill country.
ISBN 1 85284 202 4 272pp

A NORTHERN COAST TO COAST WALK *Terry Marsh*
The most popular LD walk in Britain, from St Bees to Robin Hood's Bay. Includes accommodation guide.
ISBN 1 85284 126 5 280pp

LAKE DISTRICT AND MORECAMBE BAY

A LAKE DISTRICT ANGLER'S GUIDE *Laurence Tetley*
Following his successful guide for anglers in Yorkshire the author gives full details for fishing in the Lake District. Clubs, shops, permits etc. - an indispensable guide.
ISBN 1 85284 283 0 248pp

THE CUMBRIA WAY AND ALLERDALE RAMBLE   *Jim Watson*

A guide to two popular Lake District long distance walks done in Jim's inimitable style. Includes the 75 mile Cumbria Way from Carlisle to Ulverston, and the 50 mile Allerdale Ramble from Seathwaite north-west to Grune Point.
ISBN 1 85284 242 3

THE EDEN WAY   *Charlie Emett*

A walk through part of Cumbria, following the R. Eden from Carlisle to Kirkby Stephen. Can be broken into sections by using the Settle-Carlisle railway.
ISBN 1 85284 040 4 192pp

CONISTON COPPER MINES: A Field Guide   *Eric G. Holland*

For mine explorers and the visitor or hill walker.
ISBN 0 902363 36 0 120pp

SHORT WALKS IN LAKELAND   *Aileen & Brian Evans*

Book 1: SOUTH LAKELAND *ISBN 1 85284 144 3 328pp*
Book 2: NORTH LAKELAND *ISBN 1 85284 232 6 328pp*
Book 3: WEST LAKELAND *ISBN 1 85284.308 X*
Around 60 walks in each book, on the lower fells and dales, described, mapped and illustrated in detail. Highly acclaimed. Book 2 was OWG/COLA Best Guidebook 1997

SCRAMBLES IN THE LAKE DISTRICT   *R.B. Evans*

ISBN 0 902363 39 5 192pp PVC cover

MORE SCRAMBLES IN THE LAKE DISTRICT   *R.B. Evans*

ISBN 1 85284 042 0 200p PVC cover
Exciting rock scrambles in gills or up crags to thrill the mountaineer.

SOUTH LAKELAND CYCLE RIDES   *Jennifer Richards*

21 circular cycle routes for all the family. Graded from easy to challenging, using quiet roads and tracks.
ISBN 1 85284 294 6

THE TARNS OF LAKELAND VOL I: WEST   *John & Anne Nuttall*

ISBN 1 85284 171 0 240pp

THE TARNS OF LAKELAND VOL 2: EAST   *John & Anne Nuttall*

Lakeland Book of the Year prize winner 1996. Walks to delectable tarns. Illustrated with superb drawings.
ISBN 1 85284 210 5 200pp

WALKING ROUND THE LAKES   *John & Anne Nuttall*

The ideal walk encompassing all the major summits, yet with high and low level alternatives. 145 miles in 15 stages.
ISBN 1 85284 099 4 240pp

WALKS IN THE SILVERDALE/ARNSIDE AONB   *R.B. Evans*

A well-illustrated guide to short walks in this delightful area on the fringe of the Lake District. Fully revised.
ISBN 0 902363 78 6 168pp

WINTER CLIMBS IN THE LAKE DISTRICT   *Bob Bennett, Bill Birkett, Brian Davison*

Packed with the latest routes which confirm the area as a major winter climbing venue when conditions allow.
ISBN 1 85284 246 6 200pp PVC

NORTH-WEST ENGLAND

WALKING IN CHESHIRE   *Carl Rogers*
   30 walks to suit all abilities in this diverse landscape.
   ISBN 1 85284 153 2 140pp

FAMILY WALKS IN THE FOREST OF BOWLAND   *Jack Keighley*
   30 walks written and illustrated in the author's unique manner.
   ISBN 1 85284 251 2 72pp Wire bound

WALKING IN THE FOREST OF BOWLAND   *Gladys Sellers*
   Despite the limited access in this AONB moorland area, these 30 beautiful walks take best advantage
   of the area. Packed with history and good maps.
   ISBN 1 85284 154 0 168pp

CANAL WALKS, Vol 1: North   *Dennis Needham*
   A guide to some short walks following the canal network.
   ISBN 1 85284 148 6 176pp

LANCASTER CANAL WALKS   *Mary Welsh*
   A guide to circular walks based on the canal, beautifully illustrated by Christine Isherwood.
   ISBN 1 85284 138 9 120pp A5

A WALKER'S GUIDE TO THE LANCASTER CANAL   *Robert Swain*
   Preston to Kendal, including the branch to Glasson Dock, together with the fascinating history of
   the canal.
   ISBN 1 85284 055 2 124pp

WALKS FROM THE LEEDS-LIVERPOOL CANAL   *Mary Welsh*
   34 circular walks based on the canal. Illustrated by Christine Isherwood's superb drawings.
   ISBN 1 85284 212 1 144pp

THE RIBBLE WAY   *Gladys Sellers*
   This 70 mile walk from sea to source close to a junction with the Pennine Way.
   ISBN 1 85284 107 9 112pp

WALKS IN RIBBLE COUNTRY   *Jack Keighley*
   30 family walks, with maps and diagrams all beautifully drawn.
   ISBN 1 85284 284 9 72pp   spiral binding.

WALKING IN LANCASHIRE   *Mary Welsh*
   39 walks described on a seasonal basis. Illustrated superbly by David Macaulay and Linda Waters.
   ISBN 1 85284 191 5 160pp A5 size

WALKS ON THE WEST PENNINE MOORS
- A companion guide to the recreation area   *Gladys Sellers*
   A guide to the popular Lancashire Pennines. 40 short walks, and suggestions for 4 longer walks.
   ISBN 0 902363 92 1 192pp

WALKS IN LANCASHIRE WITCH COUNTRY   *Jack Keighley*
   30 family walks with maps and diagrams all beautifully drawn.
   ISBN 1 85284 093 5 72pp spiral binding.

NOTES

NOTES

EXPLORE THE WORLD
WITH A CICERONE GUIDE

Cicerone publishes over 280 guides for walking, trekking, climbing and exploring the UK, Europe and worldwide. Cicerone guides are available from outdoor shops, quality book stores and from the publisher.

Cicerone can be contacted on
Tel. 01539 562069
Fax: 01539 563417
www.cicerone.co.uk